Brilliant and Pragmatic! – Captain George "Bc
perfect blueprint for any leader and organization wishing to embed a high
trust, high performance culture. Aside from the book being an exhilarating
read, with jaw-dropping accounts of the speed and precision embraced by the
Blue Angels, this book is full of highly practical building blocks for the creation
of high trust. The lessons contained within can be applied from the board room
to the shop floor. This should be required reading for leaders at all levels.

~ John Collingwood
Global Head of Executive Leadership, Johnson and Johnson Inc.

A Recipe for Success – This book should be mandatory reading for every
high school senior, boss, subordinate, businessperson, doctor, lawyer,
politician, parent, athlete, coach, and anyone striving for excellence in life. Mr.
Dom masterfully presents a timeless recipe for success, offering practical, real-
world lessons…Written in an engaging and accessible style…It far exceeded
my expectations…exceptionally well done!

~ Bags

The best book I've ever read on leadership! – This is a must-read book
for anyone looking to improve their relationships professionally or personally.
So many gems in this book that I will carry with me. I have read many books
on leadership and this is the best! Loved the behind the scenes look into the
Blue Angels' ready room and cockpit. I was so impressed with this book that I
sent copies of this book my sons who are beginning their careers in the Navy.

~ RF

Definitely Worth the Read (and the Price) – I enjoyed reading High
Trust Leadership. Not only that, but as I read it, I was pleasantly surprised to
realize that it was giving me the answer to a real-life issue I've recently been
trying to solve at work. That issue involves a small group of smart, successful
people who have nevertheless been exhibiting some workplace issues. And as I
read this book it jumped off the page that it's been an absence of real trust
within and among the group that is the source of those issues.

–Peter Carroll

The Perfect Wayfinder For Your Leadership Journey – Leadership exists at all levels (Individual contributor, C-level executive, family member, friend, or even stranger) and rarely have I come across a book that is applicable to every leader. If you are even remotely interested in being a better leader tomorrow than you are today, you need to read this book. If your team or organization has some level of dysfunction, this book can help you…His reflection questions are very thought provoking and his "training exercises" will help readers apply concepts directly to their roles and lives. Make time to read this book and create your own personal action plan. The path won't be easy, but it will be worth the investment.

~ Michael C. Markiewicz

Infinitely actionable! – The author has a unique perspective on leadership, having been the commander of the Blue Angels as well as holding many other leadership roles in the Navy and the business world. He clearly knows what he's talking about and I love how infinitely ACTIONABLE the book is. He doesn't talk about trust as a nebulous concept, but gives you tactical, practical steps for creating more trust in both your professional and personal lives. And I loved the "behind the scenes" stories of his time flying with the Navy. A great read!

~ Jenny Evans

A MUST READ for Leaders and Everyone – There are a lot of books about leadership out there, but I believe this one stands apart and above, as it provides a proven playbook for how to become an extraordinary leader and person, and how to deepen connections with everyone that matters in our lives. Whether you are a leader, coach, spouse/partner or parent, you will likely find yourself referring back to the practical and actionable strategies and exercises provided by Captain George Dom. I have followed his work with great admiration over the years and am thrilled to now have this book to help me in my ongoing quest to become a better leader with my team and strengthen relationships with everyone who matters in my life.

~ CKenney

THE 5 PILLARS OF TRUST

HIGH-TRUST LEADERSHIP

BUILDING HIGH PERFORMANCE TEAMS

CAPTAIN GEORGE DOM

FOREWORD BY DR. JIM LOEHR

Founder, Human Performance Institute

High Trust Leadership: Building High Performance Teams

WISE
MEDIA GROUP

rev 24-1204

TABLE OF CONTENTS

DEDICATION

To my father, LCDR William T. Dom III, USNR, a citizen sailor who selflessly answered America's call to defeat fascist aggression in the Mediterranean and the Pacific during World War II "because I never wanted anyone to be able to say I didn't do my part."

To all my Blue Angels teammates, your dedication to our mission and each other continues to inspire me.

FOREWORD

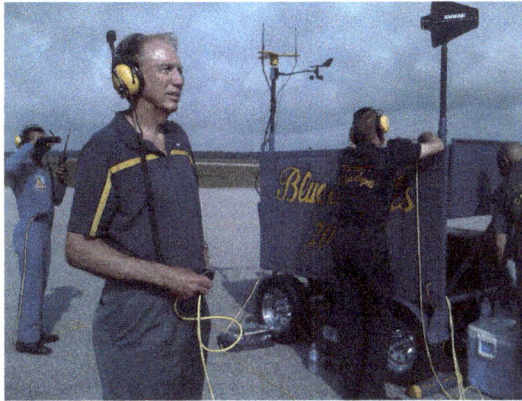

Figure 1 - Dr. Loehr watching Blue Angels practice

When George Dom invited me into the culture of the Blue Angels, I was ecstatic. And I was just as mesmerized as I had been as a young boy, filled with the thunderous joy I experienced at every Blue Angel airshow I attended with my family.

As a performance psychologist, I've worked in many high stress, extreme environments, but I was completely unprepared for and shocked by the Blue Angels. My understanding of team dynamics, risk tolerance, leadership, precision under pressure, trust, unconscious competence, full engagement, commitment to a noble mission, character, and the importance of honest, straightforward communication was changed forever. And this was not my first experience working with and learning from elite military teams.

For example, I was flown onto the deck of the USS Harry Truman aircraft carrier in a V-22 Osprey, witnessed numerous day and night landings from the carrier deck, observed brave men and women putting themselves repeatedly in harm's way, and deck officers making life and death decisions moment to moment. When I flew off the carrier in a COD aircraft (Carrier Onboard Delivery), I concluded that this high-performance culture represented the absolute zenith of teamwork, courage, precision under pressure, leadership, and commitment to excellence. However, after my experience with the Blue Angels, I realized their culture took these traits and values to an even higher level of excellence. I can say quite honestly that my time with the Blues was the single greatest learning experience of my entire career.

The formal name of the Blue Angels is the US Navy Flight Demonstration Squadron. Formed in 1946 by the Chief of Naval Operations, Admiral Chester Nimitz, the mission of the Blue Angels is to showcase the pride and professionalism of the United States Navy and Marine Corp by inspiring a culture of excellence and service to America through demonstrations and community outreach. A sobering statistic highlights the risk involved in what the Blues do day-in and day-out: a total of 26 pilots have died during training or airshow accidents in the 78 years they have been performing formation flight demonstrations. It's important to point out that the majority of those deaths occurred in the early years of the squadron's history. With increasingly advanced training protocols, more precise training methods, and strict adherence to safety measures, the fatality rate in recent history has vastly improved. However, the fact remains that significant risk still exists. Flying up to speeds of nearly 700 mph, conducting aerobatic maneuvers with only 18–24 inches separating wingtips, and doing so in winds and afternoon thermals over unfamiliar terrain demand nearly superhuman skills and teamwork.

As impressive as the six demonstration pilots are, they are the tip of the iceberg of this world-class example of organizational excellence. The Blue Angels are a team of 125 professionals in aircraft maintenance, logistics, public affairs, medical, administration, and training. Their 2–3-year assignments to the Blues results in an astounding 50% annual turnover among the 16 officers and 33% turnover among the 109 enlisted personnel!

When clients ask me how to build a truly extraordinary, high-performance culture, my answer is always the same: study the Blue Angels.

Whether the application is business, sports, or the military, the Blues have built a tested blueprint for taking human performance to unprecedented levels of excellence. I've learned that culture is everything in high performance, and with the right culture, amazing things are possible. And that's what **HIGH-TRUST** Leadership is all about. It's a deep dive into the cultural blueprint that enables the Blues to produce performance magic. Issues of purpose, mission, accountability, humility, deep trust, unconscious competence, total commitment, and authentic communication through the prism of the Blue Angel's culture represents the essence of this book. It's about the lessons learned since 1946 from the most performance demanding culture I've experienced in my life.

I strongly believe if you want to learn something truly important and challenging, you should seek out the best possible source in that space. The qualifier is tested, demonstrated excellence, year after year. Learning from the best is the shortest path to becoming the best. And, in my experience, the Blue Angels represent the best high-performance culture to learn from, bar none.

Anyone seeking to build a world class team and a world class performance culture should find this book intoxicating.

– Dr. Jim Loehr

PREFACE

In my 26-year Navy career, I flew Navy strike-fighters as a carrier air wing strike leader, TOPGUN instructor, F/A-18 squadron commander, commanding officer/flight leader of the Blue Angels, and air wing commander on the USS Dwight D. Eisenhower and USS John F. Kennedy.[1] I logged over 5,000 hours in Navy jets and I completed more than 1,000 aircraft carrier landings. Not bad for someone who considers himself an average pilot. My simple secret? What I lacked in natural ability, I overcame by hard work and dedication to earn the trust of everyone I worked and flew with. I struggled mightily at times: I almost quit during flight school, and I made many mistakes along the way. Thankfully, I was blessed to serve with principled role models who showed me how to succeed through their personal examples and willingness to let me learn from my setbacks.

After leaving the military and joining the business world, people frequently asked about our planning, organization, and training in naval aviation. The key to success in every strike-fighter squadron and aircraft carrier where I served—whether in peacetime or during combat, at TOPGUN, and in the Blue Angels—was a culture based on **HIGH-TRUST**. Trust was never assumed to be the inevitable byproduct of putting talented people together. Rather, it was a core value and strategic imperative. We recruited for it. We trained to build it every

---

[1] TOPGUN's official name is the U.S. Navy Fighter Weapons School. TOPGUN trains Strike-Fighter Tactics Instructors (SFTI) in graduate-level tactics in USN and USMC air warfare.

day. If you had it, you were rewarded and promoted. If you lost it and couldn't regain it quickly, you were sidelined or gone.

Soon, I found myself speaking to leaders of various organizations across the U.S., including the public, private, for-profit, and non-profit sectors. My thoughts on HIGH-TRUST leadership and teamwork resonated with all of them—from fast-paced, aggressive sales teams to senior leaders in the tech sector, blue collar plant managers, law enforcement, insurance companies, sports teams, and many others.

At the same time, I watched the levels of trust in all dimensions of modern life erode to the lowest levels in my lifetime: politicians and public figures, media companies, government and religious institutions, police, public health officials, sports, science, and our elected officials all suffer from low levels of public trust. We're in a trust crisis that has resulted in extreme polarization, cynicism, and disillusionment.

Nevertheless, every crisis presents an opportunity. Individuals and organizations who do the hard work to build and sustain high levels of trust will break out of the pack and enjoy great success, both individually and collectively.

Everything I learned about leadership and teamwork to excel in the air as a military flight leader and commanding officer is readily applicable on the ground, in businesses, families, and communities. Building and sustaining cultures and relationships of HIGH-TRUST is where the magic happens.

Let's get on with it.

INTRODUCTION

Figure 2 - Blue Angels 6-plane Delta formation

Imagine six F/A-18 strike-fighter pilots: four flying together in perilously close aerobatic formations while two solo pilots conduct a series of violent maneuvers with near head-on collisions at 1,000 mph of closure, operating in complete unison, literally placing their lives in each other's hands, nearly every day of the year. This extreme performance occurs safely, up close and personal, below the skyscrapers, down at treetop level, in front of millions of spectators annually. Buffeted by winds and dueling with hot summer afternoon thermals, these six pilots—and their dedicated traveling support team—push their limits every day: growing, learning, adapting, seeking perfection.

When flying just a couple feet apart at 300, 400, 500 mph at very low altitude performing three-dimensional aerobatics in formation, the wingmen aren't looking around enjoying the scenery. They are intently focused on the jet in front of them to avoid colliding while making small, timely corrections to stay in position. There are no fancy computers; it's all old-fashioned eye-hand coordination and steely concentration for 40 intense minutes of flying. During my two years flying the Blue Angels' #1 jet, I never forgot the tragic mishap suffered by the USAF Thunderbirds on January 18, 1982, while practicing a formation looping maneuver. Flying only a few feet apart, the wingmen were totally focused on the leader's jet. When the flight leader didn't pull out soon enough to complete the loop, all four fighter jets impacted the desert floor, symmetrically spaced, tragically killing all four pilots.

For our team to be successful flying Blue Angel maneuvers, I had to earn and maintain the unconditional trust of my wingmen—and they with me and each other—such that we would enthusiastically take to the sky six days a week throughout the year to push the limits of human capability. What would it take to build such a high level of trust? And what can we learn that could be applied to ALL our relationships—at work, at home, and with everyone we care about?

Looking back, I realized that my wingmen were asking five simple questions about me as their leader. Depending on the answers, they'd make a conscious or unconscious decision about how much to trust me. I believe your team, your prospects, your clients, your families, and your friends are consciously or unconsciously asking these same five questions about you:

Character — "Do you walk your talk?"
Commitment — "Will you be with us when times are tough?"
Competence — "Are you skilled and relevant?"
Connection — "Do you understand me?"
Communication — "Can I understand you?"

As we journey through the exploration of trust, these five pillars will serve as our guideposts, illuminating the path to understanding the intricate dynamics that make trust the foundation of success that elevates the performance of leaders and teams to the pinnacle of precision and excellence. The lessons I share to help you proactively build and maintain a high level of enduring trust are far from the complex, esoteric prescriptions of academics and 9-to-5 leaders. Mine are born out of the extreme and unforgiving environments of long deployments on aircraft carriers at sea, deadly air combat missions, and high-speed, close-formation jet aerobatics at very low altitudes. The lessons are hard-won in these environments because there is no room for compromise. To be effective, they must be simple and straight-forward, and they must work. But that doesn't mean they are easy.

The principles in this book apply to all leaders and teams, including businesses, government agencies, sports teams, and organizations, as well as families and couples—literally anywhere that relationships are important, because trust is the psychological water in which all relationships swim.

Although the Blue Angels are an iconic example of the highest level of human teamwork and precision, spectators often miss the essence of the Blue Angels because they make it look too easy. The profound insight on display is a team of common people achieving far beyond what they originally believed was possible by fully committing to building and sustaining an uncommon level of trust.

In this book, I will help you build trust proactively and authentically. There are no shortcuts. But with a focus on five universal principles and dedicated effort, you will learn and grow as a HIGH-TRUST Leader. It's not quick and easy. The path is not always straight forward. It's not "set it and forget it." Building trust takes time, effort, and intention. And it's worth it, because the results and benefits can be profound. It also provides a method to evaluate when NOT to trust a person or an organization, which is critically important when hiring, promoting, or considering a partnership or acquisition.

My HIGH-TRUST framework provides the building blocks to establish the foundation for individual and collective high performance. Throughout this book, I describe each pillar in general terms with illustrations to help convey my meaning. Then, I offer exercises you can apply immediately. Each one of the five pillars of trust can be viewed and studied in much greater depth. Take character. Philosophers, teachers, parents, and coaches have written and spoken about the importance of an honorable character for millennia. Although the material in this book stays at a foundational level, I hope you use it as a springboard for further study, as each dimension of trust is a rich and rewarding topic for investigation. But first, begin by applying each principle in small, daily doses and you will enjoy the benefit and satisfaction of authentically deepening every relationship in your life.

CHAPTER 1
WHAT IS TRUST?

Figure 3 - "Boss" Dom climbing into the #1 jet

Trust is the emotional glue
that holds teams together.

As I climbed the ladder of my F/A-18 Hornet and settled onto the ejection seat for my first airshow as Blue Angel #1, I marveled at the training process that prepared me for this moment. A hundred intense training flights and innumerable hours of study, briefings, and candid post-flight debriefs. My cockpit was meticulously set up by my crew chief, AO1(AW) Derrick Robinson, USN.[2] Every

---

[2] AO1(AW) stands for Aviation Ordnanceman Petty Officer 1st Class (Air Warfare).

switch in the right place, my flight gloves on the glare shield, the parachute harness and seat restraints ready to buckle-in. So familiar. No distractions. Perched next to me on the canopy rail, Petty Officer "Robbie" Robinson handed me my helmet. I slipped it on, adjusted the boom mic, and lowered the gold visor. As we shook hands, Robbie said, as he always did, "Boss, have a good one!" This brief ritual epitomized the special relationship between Blue Angel pilots and their crew chiefs. In over 40 years of military and civilian flying, my two years as a Blue Angel was the only time I didn't perform a preflight inspection of my aircraft. The crew chiefs ensured the jets were ready to fly and we trusted them completely.

DEFINING TRUST

Trust can be a fuzzy concept. It's dynamic, continually tested, and changes depending on many variables. You can be trusted by some, but not by others. You can be trusted in some areas, but not in others. But for Navy SEALs, Blue Angels, aircraft carrier pilots, high performance sports teams, Olympians and their coaches, a young child and its mother, trust isn't fuzzy or touchy-feely, it is real and tangible.

At its core, trust is a willingness to be vulnerable with our physical safety, our feelings, our finances, and our success.

Willing to be vulnerable means your success depends to some degree on someone else. It is inherently necessary in any lasting relationship and especially in a team setting. Let's face it, nothing of significance is accomplished in any sphere of life without the support and help of others. Even world-class solo performers require a cadre of supporters to propel them to new records and achievements. No one can do it alone.

But vulnerability does not mean weakness.

Think of great NFL quarterbacks like Joe Montana, Steve Young, Aaron Rogers, Tom Brady, Brett Favre, John Elway, Patrick Mahomes. Does anyone think of them as being weak? Yet their success depended on their willingness to be vulnerable—at the beginning of every play, they are handed the football and concentrate on the play opening before them, bringing all their athletic talent to bear while exposing themselves to ferocious opponents who want to tackle them with the highest possible velocity. They trust their teammates will protect them. Is that weakness?

TRUST IS A PASSPORT

Trust is the key that unlocks deeper connections with those who really matter to us. Think of it like a passport—not to enter a foreign country, but as a special invitation to places where you're not automatically accepted.[3] In relationships, it's the green light people give you to enter their world, share their thoughts, discuss their struggles, and permission to give them advice and feedback.

If you want to be let into someone's life and truly connect with them, you need to earn their trust passport. It's not a physical document, but an emotional visa that comes from genuine interactions. The journey to earning their trust can be boiled down to three key questions. These questions encompass all the things people think about before deciding whether to open up to you:

> **Can I feel safe with you?** If I show you my mistakes, will you still see me in a positive light or will you judge me? Will you give me a chance or assume the worst without listening to me?

---

[3] The idea of trust as a passport comes from a May 26, 2021 blog post by Ken Sande, rw360.org.

Do you really care about me or are you simply going through the motions? Do you have a genuine desire to assist me? Will you take the time to hear me out? Will you be there for me when I need you?

Are you capable of addressing my issues? How are you handling your own struggles and challenges? Have you been successful in tackling similar problems?

Too many leaders mistakenly think they were issued a passport with their promotion or their new title. Too many parents think they were automatically granted a passport with their child's birth certificate.

Be a HIGH-TRUST Leader: Earn your passports to the hearts and minds of those who matter. And don't let them expire through neglect.

TRUST IS THE AIR THAT ALL RELATIONSHIPS BREATHE

Trust is the air that breathes life into all great relationships. When trust is high, the air is sparkling clean and clear, and relationships flourish. When trust is low, relationships become hazy and tentative, with gasps of misunderstanding and pangs of disconnection. If the air becomes toxic with mistrust, the relationship perishes.

Like fish, who don't think about the water they swim in, we don't often think about trust proactively. When we do think about trust, it is usually in the context of damage control.

> No trust, no collaboration.
> No trust, no positive influence.
> No trust, no leadership.
> No trust, no teamwork.
> No trust, no intimacy.
> No trust, no love.

But what if we thought about trust in a new way? About intentionally and proactively developing trust to seek its extraordinary benefits? How cool would it be if:

- Everyone calms down during a crisis because you've arrived.

- Your name came up during discussions about seizing a terrific new opportunity.

- Your child's first thought when facing a crisis is to get your advice.

- You could make even your very best relationships even better!

What if we worked on the level of trust in our most important relationships proactively on a daily basis? How many people do you deeply trust? What if you had five or six more? What difference would that make?

Here's the best part: trust is infinite. No matter how good your team or your relationships are now, you can make them even better by deepening the level of trust. There is always more room to grow the relationship. No one was ever faulted for being too trustworthy.

But measuring your own trustworthiness is tricky:

- We may be trusted by some, but not by others.

- We can be trusted today, but not tomorrow.

- We often judge our own trustworthiness based on the person who trusts us most. Too often we think that if we're trusted by one, we should be trusted by all. "John trusts me, therefore, I'm trustworthy. Bob doesn't trust me, so he must have trust issues."

Chapter 2
The Trust Continuum

In order to be trusted, you
must be trustworthy.

Trust is not binary, yes or no, black or white. It is analog, complex, and dynamic; it is a continuum. We are at different places on others' trust continuum depending on our interactions with them. You may be trusted by some but not others; you may be trusted in some areas, but not in others; you may be trusted at some times but not others.

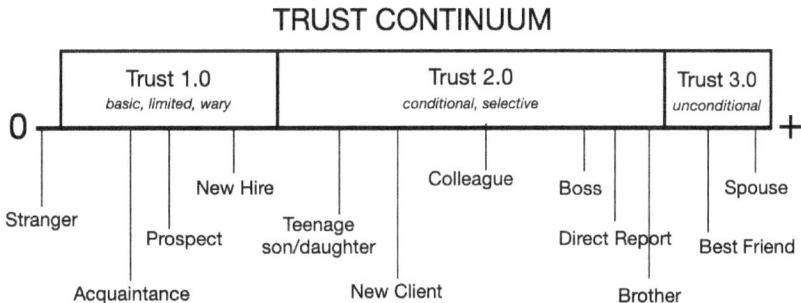

TRUST CONTINUUM

Trust 1.0 basic, limited, wary	Trust 2.0 conditional, selective	Trust 3.0 unconditional

0 ——— +

Stranger
Acquaintance
Prospect
New Hire
Teenage son/daughter
New Client
Colleague
Boss
Direct Report
Brother
Best Friend
Spouse

27

TRUST 1.0: BASIC TRUST

This is your garden-variety trust. You have a basic level of trust in someone because they have a college degree, certification, had a similar job, or were referred by your cousin. Or you assess trust based on past performance. Think about it: Why do you trust other drivers to stay on their side of a painted yellow line? Why do you trust an airliner to fly seven miles above the ground in frigid temperatures and bad weather? How about that new guy who just joined your team? And how quickly do you question your trust when the car ahead swerves slightly, the airplane is jolted by turbulence, or the new guy behaves in an odd way?

I joined the Blue Angels as the commanding officer and flight leader after commanding a fleet F/A-18 squadron embarked on the USS Dwight D. Eisenhower. I had significantly more flight time, more aircraft carrier landings, and more air combat experience than my new wingmen, but I didn't have any Blue Angels experience. As we began our preseason training, Major Pat "Kato" Cooke, Blue Angel #2, said, "Boss, study the procedures, fly your jet safely, and we'll work together to have you ready to lead the flight demonstration." I was at Trust 1.0 and the beginning of my journey.

Learning to Talk and Fly

Flying on and off aircraft carriers, naval aviators take pride in minimizing radio transmissions, and for good reason: a critical radio call could be missed if someone is chattering on the frequency. The combination of standard procedures, a thorough preflight briefing, and the disciplined use of defined terminology to minimize misunderstandings allows for complex tactics and procedures to be conducted with little-to-no radio communication. For example, during daylight operations, naval aviators routinely land 15–20 jets on aircraft carriers every 45 seconds without a single radio transmission! It's called a "zip-lip" recovery. Even at night, we can land a jet every 60 seconds with minimal transmissions.

Blue Angels communications are quite different. In order to fly within a couple feet of each other while turning, rolling, and looping in formation, the leader must make routine transmissions on the radio. Before I moved the throttles or the control stick in my cockpit, I gave my wingmen a preparatory radio call followed by a call to execute. To roll the formation, I'd say, "OK," but drawn out a bit: "OooooooK." The "Ooooo" was preparatory, and on the "K," we'd all move the sticks in our cockpits to the left in unison and the jets would roll to the left with the wingmen making small, continuous corrections to stay in position. On the first few days of learning to talk and fly, after moving the controls without first making the correct radio call, I quickly realized I had a long way to go.

At this point, our team was at Trust 1.0. We trusted each other to fly safely, but we were only doing basic maneuvers with wide separation because we hadn't yet demonstrated the consistency necessary to earn greater trust.

TRUST 2.0: CONDITIONAL AND SELECTIVE TRUST

Conditional trust is where people spend most of their time (i.e., "If you do A, B, and C, I'll trust you with D."). For example, in the business world, contracts artificially raise the level of trust by lowering the level of vulnerability. They explain what each party is responsible for and state what will happen if either party doesn't meet the letter of the contract. Alternately, there is selective trust "I trust you with this, but not with that."

We worked very hard during Winter Training, memorizing the standard Blue Angel procedures and terminology and the various maneuver profiles and parameters, with exhausting repetition during each flight. As we improved, we tightened the formations, lowered the altitudes, and introduced more dynamic maneuvers.

As the Commanding Officer and Flight Leader, I thought of Bill Russell, who coached and played on the NBA's Boston Celtics championship teams in the 1960s. Not only did I have all the responsibilities of being the squadron's commanding officer, but I also had to don my flight suit, climb in the jet, and lead the formation every day. My job was to fly as smoothly and consistently as humanly possible every single day to allow my wingmen to fly to Blue Angels standards.

When I was the commanding officer of a fleet squadron, I could pick and choose my flights, but with the Blues, I had no choice but to fly every flight. If one of the wingmen couldn't fly, we'd fly a 5-plane practice or show. If I couldn't fly, none of us would fly. In my two years on the team, I missed one practice flight due to illness.

As we completed Winter Training and began the airshow season, we had done the hard work to develop the HIGH-TRUST culture necessary to put on a Blue Angels airshow, to fly to the highest standards set by all the teams beginning in 1946. But we still had a ways to go. By then, I was at conditional Trust 2.0—I could fly a Blue Angels airshow, but I was operating with all the procedures and maneuvers in cognitive conscious memory. My wingmen were wary that a distraction could negatively affect my performance with significant consequences.

TRUST 3.0: UNCONDITIONAL TRUST

By mid-season in July, we had gelled as a Team. Everyone had mastered their roles at every level of the squadron. We were no longer climbing into our jets; we were strapping them on. Many of the procedures and details we needed to fly the demo had moved from conscious to unconscious memory. Having invested in our relationships with each other during weeks on the road at different show sites and weather conditions each weekend, we moved from Trust 2.0 to 3.0.

Trust 3.0 is when you've done the work, made the investments in time, consistency, transparency, connection, and communication to reach a point in a relationship where the other person feels unconditional trust and thinks, "I trust you, period."

Trust 2.0 feels transactional, like a contract. You wonder, "What do they want from me?" "What do I need to do?" "What will it take to make this work?"

Trust 3.0 is transformational. "What do they have for me?" It's values-based: "What should I do?" "I feel safe to be myself, my real self; not play a role, not hide some of my cards."

Trust 3.0 is a covenant between people.

We moved the formations to their tightest positions and continued to lower the altitudes of the maneuvers. At this point in the season, I could:

- Accurately judge altitude by the colors and textures on the ground.

- Discern the effect of wind at different altitudes during a maneuver and adjust the template of our airshow profiles to fit the local terrain and buildings.

- Feel when my wingmen were in position as the airflow over their canopies pushed my wings.

- Change the trajectory of a maneuver by adjusting the inflection of my voice on the radio—not the words I said, but how I said the words.

- Pull harder than usual at the bottom of a loop to avoid a ridgeline; tighten a turn around a skyscraper; or speed the roll of the formation to stay below the clouds—and my wingmen would stay with me in tight Blue Angels formation.

As we raised our game little by little each week, it didn't get easier. It still required steely concentration as well as physically and mentally exhausting work to avoid complacency. But it was worth it.

The same was true on the ground. I proudly watched the high activity of our support personnel completing the thousands of tasks necessary to prepare the jets and do all the work behind the scenes to give the crowd a Blue Angels experience each weekend. From early morning until late at night, they worked the countless routine details, responded to surprises, and overcame every challenge with great enthusiasm and efficiency. Just like the pilots in the air, they could practically read each other's minds, knowing what needed to be done, and making it happen. It was inspiring to see them look out for one another, sharing burdens, filling in wherever needed, always punctuated with laughter and good-natured ribbing.

The magic of **HIGH-TRUST** requires continuous work, sacrifice, and diligence. And when people are involved, progress is not a straight line. It's never "set it and forget it." We had to work on it every day, and as the leader, I had to set an example, which is often humbling.

TRUST 2.0 vs. 3.0

Wariness vs. Anticipation

Trust 2.0, there is a sense of wariness, "What did I miss in the contract?", "What will I do if he does the very minimum, but not the level of quality or excellence that we discussed?" "What does she want from me?"

Trust 3.0, there are pleasant surprises as the result of compounding everyone's efforts. Synergy, creativity, and collaboration are unleashed. There is eager anticipation: "I can't wait to see the progress we make today," and, "What does she have for me?"

Rules-based vs. Values-based

Trust 2.0 is rules-based. While parsing the words in the contract to protect yourself, you wonder, "What am I required to do?"

Trust 3.0 is values-based, "What is the right thing to do?"

Pragmatic vs. Principled

Trust 2.0 is a pragmatic mindset, "What will work?" "What is good enough?"

Trust 3.0 is a principled mindset, "Does this fulfill the spirit of our agreement?"

Transactional vs. Transformational

Trust 2.0 feels transactional; it's a contract, a quid pro quo.

Trust 3.0 is transformational; it's a covenant, with a sum much greater than its parts.

At Trust 3.0, everyone feels safe to be themselves, their real selves, and bring their whole selves to work every day. They accept responsibility for their performance and don't shy away from admitting their mistakes to preserve trust and help others avoid the same. More on this later in the postflight debrief.

TRAINING TO BUILD TRUST

The thing most people miss when they leave the military is the deep feeling of being able to trust the person next to them. They knew they could depend on their teammates to carry out the mission in accordance with what they're supposed to do. Lives depended on it. Once you've experienced that level of trust as the norm, you never forget it.

We can develop that same feeling of trust in business, government, communities, and families. We can be better and do more through trust. We have the tools. We just have to practice. And it is never too late for training, especially leadership training. In the military we're all about training. Because it works.

So, how do we proactively train for leadership?

When it comes to the big stuff, I believe we will do the right thing when everyone is watching—but what about the little things every day? That's where we can really make a difference.

TRAINING EXERCISE: LOW TRUST VS. HIGH TRUST

Grab a pen and paper or open a Word document. Let's do some writing to slow down, focus, and reflect on your experiences with low trust and high trust situations.

Exploring Low Trust

Step 1: Identify a time when you were on a team or in a relationship with very low trust.

Step 2: Reflect on that situation. Think about where you were, who you were with, and what happened.

Step 3: How did that low-trust situation feel? Describe it.

Step 4: What was the effect of low trust? What happened—or didn't happen—because there was very little trust?

STOP here until you have written answers to the prompts and questions above.

I've asked these questions of hundreds of people. The words most often used to describe the feelings when there is low trust or mistrust:

> Afraid and Anxious
> Frustrated
> Marginalized
> Angry
> Unappreciated
> Defensive
> Micro-managed
> Sad and Cynical
> Disengaged and Apathetic

And the effects of a low trust environment:

> Depleted and burned-out
> Turf battles
> Politics and keeping score

Guarded communications
No loyalty
"It's a job"
Slow — Everything seems hard
Lousy retention
Divorce!

Exploring *HIGH-TRUST*

Step 1: Identify a time when you were on a team, or in a relationship, with very high trust.

Step 2: Reflect on that situation. Think about where you were, who you were with, what happened.

Step 3: How did that HIGH-TRUST situation feel? Describe it.

Step 4: What was the effect of HIGH-TRUST? What happened—or didn't happen—because there was very high trust?

STOP here until you've written about the prompts and questions above before comparing your answers to words below.

Here are the words most often used to describe the feelings of HIGH-TRUST:

Safe
Respected
Understood
Creative
Confident
Appreciated
Challenged
Self-Directed and Autonomous

Energized and Engaged

And the results of a high trust environment:

Honesty and Candor
Accountability
Speed, Agility, Innovation
Increased Productivity
Determination and Resilience
Loyalty and Camaraderie
Fun
"Hardest work I've ever done"
"We were a true team"

Let's briefly address each of these feelings:

Safe. Safe to be yourself—your real self, your whole self. Safe to share your ideas, concerns, stories, hopes, fears. You don't have to wear a mask at work or play a role. You can be yourself.

Respected. You are valued, regardless of your role. Your teammates see the best in you and help you grow.

Understood. Your teammates take time and truly listen to understand you. We'll discuss this a lot more in the coming chapter on CONNECTION.

Creative. Because you are allowed to share your crazy ideas, a HIGH-TRUST culture opens the window for people to think differently, to see new patterns, and connections.

Confident. Because you feel safe to try new things, stumble, and grow, you become confident and not afraid of failing, because your teammates won't let you feel like a failure.

Appreciated. Your efforts are noticed and recognized as valuable to the team's success.

Challenged. Being given the precious gift of trust, you feel a duty not to let them down. You strive harder in order to be worthy of the gift.

Self-Directed and Autonomous. You are trusted to fulfill your duties and responsibilities in the best way possible. No one is looking over your shoulder or doing your work for you. You own it; it's yours.

Energized and Engaged. Feeling needed, respected, and appreciated, you come to work every day full of energy and the desire to knock it out of the park.

The results of a HIGH-TRUST culture:

Honesty and Candor. In a HIGH-TRUST culture, everyone feels safe to be honest with each other. No dancing around on eggshells, afraid of igniting fight-or-flight defensiveness in your teammates. But HIGH-TRUST evokes more than honesty, it inspires candor. What's the difference?

- Here's a basic depiction of honesty: I ask you a question and you tell me the truth. The problem is, if I have to ask for the truth, it slows us down and prevents us from operating at peak speed. Flying in the Blue Angels #1 jet at 500 mph, if I had to ask for the truth, it would've been too late.

- The solution is candor: tell me the truth when I need to hear it. The challenge with candor is if you allow someone to bring you the truth, you'll get it once, and depending on how you react to the truth, you may never receive it again. More on this and the need for truth-tellers ahead.

Accountability. In a HIGH-TRUST environment, people aren't afraid of the scoreboard. If they miss the target, their teammates are there to help them raise their game. My favorite definition of a team: "A group of people with a common mission who try to make each other look good."

Speed, Agility, and Innovation. In a HIGH-TRUST environment, everything moves quickly because trust is the air teams fly in. When the air is bright and clear, the team flies fast, adapts quickly to challenges and opportunities, innovating often (see Creativity above). Conversely, when the trust is low, the air is dark and toxic, everyone is wary, and progress slows.

Increased Productivity. With speed, accountability, and engagement, work is completed with a high level of both quantity and quality.

Determination and Resilience. HIGH-TRUST teams support each other, encourage each other, and help each other. They remind each other why the work they're doing is important and help each other overcome setbacks and mistakes. A low-trust team is brittle: when faced with significant adversity, everyone cowers in a defensive, self-serving posture, and inevitably, the team shatters. A HIGH-TRUST team can take a punch, come together, and grow stronger from the shared experience of overcoming adversity. More on this when we discuss COMMITMENT.

Loyalty and Camaraderie. When teammates are looking out for each other, it inspires loyalty and a willingness to give the benefit of the doubt, and to forgive mistakes. Very often, people develop strong bonds of friendship on HIGH-TRUST teams, but as you'll see later, friendship and camaraderie are not required to achieve high performance.

Fun. Hanging around trustworthy people who share a common purpose is just plain fun. Depending on the difficulty of the mission and conditions, it may not be pleasurable, but it results in a feeling of deep satisfaction.

"Hardest work I've ever done." HIGH-TRUST teammates are encouraged to get outside their comfort zone in order to learn and grow. They suffer the pangs of learning a new skill, but their engagement reaches new heights as they gain confidence and increase the level of their performance. (See "Challenged" above.)

"We were a true team." By definition, to become a HIGH-TRUST team, there has to be interdependence, coordination, and collaboration with shared purpose and sacrifice— all ingredients required for teamwork.

CHAPTER 3
TEAMWORK AND LEADERSHIP

Trust is the emotional glue that holds teams together. You can't lead if you don't have trust and you can't have trust if you don't have integrity.

—Noel Tichy and Warren Bennis[4]

TRUST AND TEAMWORK

Many people assume that trust is a straight-forward by-product of gathering smart, talented, and accomplished people. That works to some extent, but it doesn't happen naturally on its

---

[4] Noel Tichy and Warren Bennis, Judgment: How Winning Leaders Make Great Calls.

own. There are many examples of dysfunctional and underachieving teams comprised of military personnel, highly skilled athletes, and business professionals. Trust requires deliberate work with daily attention and nurturing. Just ask any successful leader of a championship team or a company that has enjoyed lasting success.

I've spoken with many CEOs and organizational leaders who lament about wanting more teamwork from their executives, their managers, their sales teams. But when I peel back the onion, it becomes obvious they are not a true team; they are a bowling team—each person stays in their lane, does their work, and earns their merit raise and bonus, without depending on anyone else for their success. It's additive, not synergistic.

In order to have teamwork, the team must be interdependent. Its members must rely on each other to achieve a common goal that is more important than individual performance.

In *The 5 Dysfunctions of a Team*, Patrick Lencioni identified the absence of trust as the fundamental problem with teams that don't work well together. He describes the five dysfunctions as:

- Absence of trust—unwilling to be vulnerable within the group, which leads to:

- Fear of conflict—seeking artificial harmony over constructive passionate debate and leads to:

- Lack of commitment—feigning buy-in for group decisions creates ambiguity throughout the organization and leads to:

- Avoidance of accountability—ducking the responsibility to call peers on counterproductive behavior which sets low standards and leads to:

- Inattention to results—focusing on personal success, status and ego before team success.

In 2012, Google launched Project Aristotle, a study that analyzed the qualities of their top-performing teams by examining hundreds of in-house teams. The data revealed that the most critical aspect for a functioning team was psychological safety, defined as a shared conviction within a team that it is safe for interpersonal risk-taking. It is characterized by a climate of trust and mutual respect, where team members are at ease being themselves without the threat of embarrassment, rejection, or punishment. Employees do not wish to put on a façade or disconnect from their personal lives when they step into the office. To cultivate a sense of psychological safety, employees need to feel confident enough to express their fears and concerns without backlash. Conversations about challenging or uncomfortable topics should be encouraged rather than focusing solely on work efficiency.

TRUST AND LEADERSHIP

While leaders come in all shapes, sizes, styles, personalities, and temperaments, successful leaders share three key characteristics:

1. **Vision.** Successful leaders see opportunities sooner and clearer than others, something bigger than themselves, something they can't accomplish alone.

2. **An unwillingness to accept the status quo.** While managers do the important work of improving the efficiency and effectiveness of current processes and procedures, leaders are driven to move the team to achieve something new, to reach new heights, to move into new areas.

3. **Influence.** Leaders can influence others to make their vision a reality.

Fundamentally, leadership is all about change, about taking people to a new level, a new place. But facilitating change is not easy, because people fear change. There is always anxiety associated with change. Successful leaders overcome this inherent fear in their followers because the leader is TRUSTED.

MEASURING TRUSTWORTHINESS

How do we measure our own level of trustworthiness? Usually by the people who trust us the most (e.g., "My best friend, Bill, trusts me, so I must be trustworthy. Fred doesn't trust me. Fred must have trust issues!").

Other people measure our trustworthiness by the only yardstick they have: *our actions and behavior.* Unfortunately, when we are faced with a situation where our actions contradict our words, we let ourselves off the hook by grading ourselves by a different yardstick: *our intentions.*

"Sorry the report is overdue. I planned to get it done today, but. . ."

"I know I promised to attend my son's basketball game, but. . ."

In the end, your assessment of your trustworthiness is interesting, but not sufficient. What matters is what score the others give you. They're measuring your trustworthiness by watching your behaviors.

WHAT'S IN IT FOR ME?

Why should you apply these lessons and principles to raise the level of trust in the relationships that matter to you? Because trust is rewarded. In 2017, one studied observed:

> Compared with low-trust companies, people at high-trust companies report 74 percent less stress, 106 percent more energy at work, 50 percent higher productivity, 13 percent fewer sick days, 76 percent more engagement, 29 percent more satisfaction with their lives, and 40 percent less burnout.[5]

Interestingly, in a March 2021 Gallup Panel survey, only 23% of U.S. employees marked "strongly agree" when asked if they trust the leadership of their organization. If we doubled that number, it would still be disturbing that so many people don't trust the most important people in their professional life.

And let's face it, we're in a trust crisis that manifests itself in nearly every dimension of modern life: Wall Street, Main Street, religious institutions, professional sports, polarized politics, and on and on. Rarely have we seen the level of trust so low across our society and around the world. But every crisis provides an opportunity, and this one is no different.

This is a huge opportunity for you and your organization. Because few, if any, are proactively building trust as a core value. What if you were

---

[5] "The Neuroscience of Trust" by Paul J. Zak, 2017, *Harvard Business Review.*

considered the most trusted person in your organization? What would that mean?

- Everyone wants YOU on their team. If there's a crisis or an opportunity, they're coming to you. They want you on their team.

- Everyone wants to be on YOUR team! If you are respected as a HIGH-TRUST leader and given an important mission, people will come out of the woodwork to join you on your quest to slay the dragon.

Trust has a power of attraction. When you are viewed as trustworthy, great people and great opportunities will gravitate to you.

When I was in flight school, I realized I wasn't the most naturally gifted pilot. So, I made it my goal that whenever someone saw my name next to theirs on the flight schedule—for training or combat—I wanted them to immediately think, "Excellent! I'm flying with Dom. Tomorrow is going to be a great flight because I can trust and depend on him."

I'll be bold enough to claim that building a HIGH-TRUST culture is THE key leadership skill in this knowledge-worker age. With it, you can enjoy the collective intelligence of your team that far surpasses adding each one individually. Without it, you'll never reach your full potential.

THE FIVE PILLARS OF HIGH-TRUST

I assumed command of the Blue Angels at a challenging time. The flight leader before me had resigned because he lost the team's trust. He could not consistently fly up to Blue Angel standards day after day, and so— to his everlasting credit—he put the team above himself and stepped aside. So, not only did I have to fly to a new level of precision and consistency, but I had to restore the trust and confidence of the entire team.

My goal was to build such a high level of trust that our team would set a new standard for Blue Angel flying and put it back at the top. This required first building **HIGH-TRUST** in me as the leader and then **HIGH-TRUST** among our entire team.

And don't get me wrong, I'm not suggesting for a minute that you should blindly trust others. Actually, I hope you'll use this framework to decide NOT to trust someone who hasn't earned it, because it's based on the axiom:

IN ORDER TO BE TRUSTED,
YOU MUST BE TRUSTWORTHY

I want you to trust trustworthy people and to not trust untrustworthy people.

People want to be trusted, and all too often it is something they expect will be given to them freely. But trust can't be expected, demanded, bought, or coerced; it is a gift, a reward that must be repeatedly earned, from the inside out.

I thought long and hard about what I needed to do to be deemed trustworthy by my teammates. Looking back on my experience during the two years I flew the Blue Angels' #1 jet, I recognized there were five interdependent, interrelated pillars of trustworthiness. What worked in the air also worked on the ground, at work, and at home. These five pillars improved every relationship I applied them to.

If we ever had an interpersonal issue, it was caused by a problem with one or more of the five pillars. The good news is every improvement in one pillar positively affects the other four. Working on each one creates an upward spiral of trust.

For each pillar, there was a question my team was asking about me every day. I believe these are the same questions being asked about you.

The five pillars of trustworthiness are: character, commitment, competence, connection and communication. The first three are foundational and build self-trust. The last two build relational trust.

Let's take 'em one by one.

CHAPTER 4
CHARACTER

Do you walk your talk?

In Navy and Marine squadrons, pilots learn to be flexible during high-tempo operations. There are often delays making final repairs to a jet, or sometimes maintenance personnel need a few more minutes to complete their preflight servicing checklists. In the two years I was a Blue Angel, every time the pilots and I arrived in Maintenance Control to review the maintenance logs and sign for the jets, we were never told that one or more jets needed more time—NEVER. And when we walked out onto the ramp, the frontman, crew chiefs, and mechs were *always* in formation in front of the jets at parade rest, ready to go. Not some of the time, not most of the time, but *every time*. This was a powerful example for the rest of us to emulate. I could only imagine the dedication, determination, and grit it took to make that happen day-in and day-out for two years. Their leadership by example was inspirational.

First is the TALK: your promises, your commitments, your responsibilities, your values. Are they positive and admirable, arousing and deserving of respect and approval from the other members of the team (or family, relationship, etc.)?

Trust is based on shared ethical values, norms, and standards. But not the ones that you simply say you have or post on the corporate lobby wall or in a fancy values statement on your website. I'm talking about your real values and standards, the ones you and your teammates really mean.

If I asked you to write down three core values—values you would truly sacrifice and suffer for—could you do it? Do the members of your team know what they are? What values do you have in common with your teammates? Are they positive, affirming, ethical? The Navy and Marine Corps share three core values: honor, courage, and commitment.

In addition to core values, our team had standards:

- Be honest and accept responsibility for your performance. No excuses.
- Accept constructive criticism as a gift to help you improve your performance.
- Every role on the team is important. Own your role and do your best. Respect others.
- We are an elite team. Strive for excellence in everything you do. Get a little better every day.
- We represent the Navy and Marine Corps 24/7/365.
- Being a Blue Angel is an extraordinary privilege.

Next is the WALK: How do others measure your trustworthiness? By the only yardstick they have: your actions. Are your actions consistent with our values and standards? Not just when it's easy, but when it's hard and inconvenient, when no one is looking, when you're tired or discouraged, when you're angry, frustrated, or in a hurry. Not just in the big things, but also in the numerous little actions of each day. If they're consistent, then you have integrity and are honorable. But if you don't, you are a hypocrite. Yep, sorry, harsh but true.

The unspoken question is, "Do you keep your promises, live our shared values, and lead by example?"

Failure to walk your talk can be born out of impatience, fatigue, distraction, frustration, anxiety, urgency, and many other short-term discomforts that cause us to compromise our integrity and reputation over the longer term. There are two key barriers to walking your talk: rationalization and blind spots.

RATIONALIZATION

When we fall short and compromise our values and standards, we measure ourselves by a different yardstick than our actions. We let ourselves off the hook by measuring ourselves by our intentions.

Rationalization may sound something like this:

- "I missed my numbers this month, but…"
- "I know I'm late for the meeting again, but…"
- "It won't hurt to cut the corner this time, because…"
- "I know I wasn't honest with you, but…"

Fill in the blanks. We're good at it. As *Seinfeld's* George Costanza once said, "It's not a lie if you believe it." And we have a highly trained ability for self-deception when our conscience is tugged by our hypocrisy. Often, others will cut us some slack for a little while based on our intentions, but sooner or later, the honeymoon is over.

(Later, in Chapter 6, I describe how my wingmen helped me come to grips with my rationalization, reframe my attitude, and dig deeper to improve my performance.)

BLIND SPOTS

No matter how perceptive you are, you can't be fully aware of how you are being perceived by others, especially by those who don't know you well or don't interact with you regularly. We all have blind spots.

Even when we think we're doing everything right there's no way even the most aware person can know how they're coming across to others. Why? Because we're not them. They come to work every day with different life experiences, different emotions, and different circumstances. You probably have a pretty good idea of how your teammates view you, but as the team gets larger and the number of interactions gets smaller, the potential for misunderstanding grows.

When my younger daughter was five years old, she was enamored with all-things Disney. She would ask me regularly if we could take a family trip to Disney World. Of course, I wanted to give her an exciting childhood experience at Disney, so I'd reply, "Yes! We'll plan a trip to Disney." At one point, my wife (my consummate truth-teller) pointed out to me, "When are you planning to go to Disney?" I replied, "Oh, I don't know, how about next Spring when work slows down?" She said, "You know, your daughter operates on a two-week time horizon. Every two weeks that goes by and no trip to Disney is a broken promise." Whoops! We headed to Disney shortly thereafter.

I have a friend in the financial services sector. He's had four different bosses in the last four years. He said, "If I am told one more time that my opinion is valued and my boss has an open-door policy, I'm going to throw-up!" I'll bet each one of his bosses meant it when they said that phrase, but their actions did not back it up.

That's why we have to have "truth-tellers" in our lives, people we give permission to tell us the truth when we need to hear it, especially when our behavior contradicts our values.

TRUTH-TELLER

As HIGH-TRUST leaders and teammates, we must cultivate a tireless desire to learn the truth. And the truth shows up in a variety of ways: from the thunderclap of a heart attack to a notice of divorce to the whisper of an off-hand remark or a puzzled look from a young teammate.

Other than your spouse and children, do you know who is the best at telling you the truth? People who don't like you very much. Because they don't care how you feel about it. Unfortunately, they'll take a kernel of truth, wrap it up in a lot of drama, and stick it in your face. HIGH-TRUST Leaders have to be wise and curious enough to listen carefully and unpack it all to see if there is something actionable that they can apply to raise their game. HIGH-TRUST leaders view the truth as a gift no matter how it shows up.

What makes a good truth-teller? In her book, *Radical Candor*, Kim Scott offers the following advice: "Find somebody you trust, who possesses wisdom, who can be painfully objective, and who has nothing to lose professionally from this relationship, and let them serve you in this role on a regular basis."

As commanding officer of an F/A-18 fleet squadron, the Blue Angels, and Carrier Air Wing Seven, I realized I wouldn't get the full picture of the issues affecting the organization through the usual communication channels. There were too many filters. So, I made it a daily habit to regularly walk among the offices and shops on the ship when we were at sea or in the hangar when ashore, sometimes during the day, sometimes at night. Just observing what was going on and spending a little time in each shop to ask how things were going. When you ask a Sailor or Marine, "How's it going?", you better be ready to hear the unvarnished truth as they see it. I made it a point to respect the chain of command and not make decisions to solve problems or complaints on the spot. I would subsequently follow up with the department heads to get their opinions and recommendations without letting my enlisted truth-tellers get caught in the middle. As I returned to my office each time, I had additional insights and perspectives into the challenges we were facing.

All political campaigns are attempts to build trust—winning the trust of voters to get elected to office. Their opponents use negative ads to degrade their perceived trustworthiness. Politicians take polls to measure their "favorability rating." If we took a poll of your teammates, what ratings would you receive?

What if I told you your trust ratings are being polled every day? They're just not published in the conventional sense. But make no mistake, everyone you know is making an ongoing assessment as a basis for their actions, responses, and willingness to trust you and your organization.

So, if they're measuring you, doesn't it make sense to proactively work to raise your numbers in an authentic, genuine way?

CHARACTER TRAINING

No one is born with good character; it's not a hereditary trait. And it isn't determined by a single noble act. If you want to build a trustworthy character, focus on your behavior over an extended period of time.

Improving behavior takes practice. If improving a physical skill (e.g., hitting a baseball, playing the piano, public speaking, flying a plane, etc.) takes practice, so does improving a character skill.

Practice integrity: walking the talk, making your actions congruent with your words, your values, your beliefs, and your team's standards.

But how can someone practice integrity? By simply paying attention to the numerous choices we all face every day to do the right thing. Don't look the other way; don't procrastinate; don't rationalize.

I once observed a teenager shoplifting. I overcame the urge to not get involved and chose to speak up because I had two daughters about her age, and if they misbehaved, I'd want someone to remind them it's wrong. It was a little thing, a tiny incident, but it was a big thing for my character practice. Looking back on it, I was surprised by how much I was inclined to look the other way, to not say anything. I was also surprised how much easier it was for me to not look the other way the next time I was faced with a similar choice. I was figuratively out on the driving range grooving my character swing.

As your character muscles grow, you'll find it easier and easier to proactively do the right thing. You'll avoid some big crises that weren't allowed to fester and grow until they suddenly explode. And when big choices are required, you'll nearly automatically respond with integrity, thanks to your training. Everyone around you will look at you differently; not because your beliefs have changed, but because your behavior has changed. Their trust and admiration will grow.

Training Exercise #1: Practice Living Your Core Values

Are you willing to look at your everyday challenges and choices as character practice? It's easier to walk your talk if you've beaten a path using small steps every day.

1. Make a list of your top 5 core values.

2. Each day, choose one value to proactively demonstrate through your behavior. Here are some examples as illustrations:

    Monday: show respect to someone who can't help or hurt you.

    Tuesday: take responsibility to solve an unexpected problem at work.

    Wednesday: look for three opportunities during the day to show kindness.

    Thursday: write a note to tell someone who goes unnoticed that you care and appreciate them.

    Friday: be a good citizen; do something to help your community.

3. Use a daily journal to track your practice. What did you learn? Are you improving in consistency and effect?

4. Rinse and repeat. Forever.

When the storm hits, we don't rise to the occasion, we fall to our training. Every action you take is moving your character needle one direction or the other. Which direction did your needle move today?

Training Exercise #2: Use Role Models to Build Your Character

1. Make a list of three people who exhibit the values you feel are important to be happy and successful. Pick the first three people that come to mind, living or dead. Preferably, they should be individuals you have known personally, but you can also choose people you have only observed or studied from a distance.

2. Next to each name, write the reason(s) you admire them. What qualities do they possess that you would like to develop in yourself? What is it about their behavior that you would like to emulate? Why do they make you feel the way they do?

3. This week, start every morning by selecting one person from the list. Set a timer for 60 seconds. Close your eyes for just one minute to see this person and imagine the two of you together. Reflect on the quality or characteristic he or she possesses and demonstrates that you admire. Plan for an opportunity to act in their way one time before lunch.

   - If you admire the person because he is kind, show kindness at least once before lunch.

   - If you admire the person because she is patient, show patience before lunch.

   - If you admire the person because they are disciplined, demonstrate discipline by doing something you know you should, but too often let yourself off the hook (e.g., pass up that sugary donut; get to the gym for a workout; make the call you've been putting off; finish the report that's been nagging you, etc.).

4. Do it again at lunch. Take one minute—just 60 seconds—to reflect on the same person. Think about them and how it made you feel when you demonstrated their admirable quality that morning. Here are some ideas to find 60 seconds for reflection in your busy, distracted day:

- If you're eating alone, do it right after the waiter has taken your order.

- If you're eating fast food or brought your lunch, do it when you take your seat.

- If you're microwaving, do it while the timer is counting down.

- If you're eating with someone, do it when they go to the restroom to wash their hands.

- If you drive to the restaurant, take a minute before getting out of your car.

5. Demonstrate this person's quality again in the afternoon. Just once. Extra credit for additional reps as you exercise your character muscle.

6. Reflect momentarily at dinner on your morning and afternoon exercise. What was it like? How did it make you feel to be more like this person? To be closer to them "in deed"?

7. Tomorrow night, when you turn off the light to go to sleep, imagine being in this person's company once more. Feel gratitude for their example and connection.

8. Repeat with the other two names on your list over the next two days.

Imagine how satisfying it would be to have others think of you when doing this exercise.

Training Exercise #3: Use a Crisis to Grow Character and Resilience

High-stress situations can provide the greatest opportunity for growth if you view them as such. In the Navy and Marine Corps, we are always training, always seeking to improve our individual and team performance. Even in combat, under the most stressful conditions, we review our performance and seek improvement.

A while back, I was engulfed in a metaphorical storm. Although there were clouds that provided some foreshadowing, the storm arrived with a thunderclap. I was practically knocked for a loop. The fight-or-flight reaction kicked in, and I was paralyzed for a short time with fear and a strong urge to flee, to give in, to avoid the pain that was sure to last for a long while.

Fortunately, I had a great truth-teller who brought me to my senses. He helped me change my perspective. Then, I faced the storm quite differently. Sure, the pain was still there, the anxiety, and some amount of fear, but I saw it as an opportunity to grow my character, to demonstrate my commitment to my family, with the expectation of emerging from the storm with greater strength and honor.

To paraphrase: I was acting as a buyer agent for a wealthy client who was acquiring his first corporate jet. When the windshield cracked on one of his first flights, he threatened to sue me despite the fault lying with the aircraft manufacturer that inspected and passed the windshield during the pre-purchase inspection. I was an easy target compared to a large corporation with deep pockets and an army of lawyers. I had performed my services in strict compliance with industry best practices and the terms of our agreement, but I was vulnerable because I couldn't afford the high cost of a protracted legal process.

Below are questions I asked myself in this situation. I hope they are helpful to you in your next storm.

1. How do I want to deal with the situation?
    a. Accept it, don't deny it. Don't think it will go away. Look at it squarely in the face without trying to wish it away or diminish its potential damage in terms of money, time, distraction, and emotional turmoil. What is the worst that can happen? What is the best? What is the most likely?

2. Develop a response plan.

    a. Mentally: What is the game I'm in? How does it work? What are my advantages and disadvantages? How do I assess the risk? How do I play the game to maximize achieving my objective while staying true to my values?

    b. Emotionally: How do I respond to avoid having the storm consume all my attention with paralyzing distraction from my other responsibilities? How do I avoid having this issue hijack my precious attention from more important subjects, especially my ability to be present? How do I deal with this in the background with minimal distraction? How do I not let it affect my confidence, my esteem, my positive emotional energy and momentum?

    c. Spiritually: How do I emerge from this life-event (e.g., financial crisis, emotional upheaval, interpersonal conflict, etc.) stronger, smarter, and with greater resilience and self-awareness? What example do I want to set? How do I want to be remembered by the people who matter to me?

3. Keep a list of lessons. This is where the benefit resides. Turn a huge challenge into a positive experience.

4. Rise above the fight-or-flight consciousness and observe this life-event in somewhat of a detached way in order to respond and adapt in accordance with your worldview and values. In other words, walk your talk; live your values. Trust yourself that you can move forward and endure the storm.

5. Here's another secret: Write about the crisis. Just 10 minutes a day for a few days will make a big difference. Write about anything and everything that comes to mind. Don't edit, don't hold back, don't judge—just write, write, write in full sentences. Extra credit if you pick up a pen and paper to handwrite in your own unique, personal font.[6]

6. Acknowledge and accept mistakes. Don't deny or discount your behavior and results. But also, don't exaggerate. No mountains from molehills. Keep evaluating to maintain a proper perspective.

7. Focus on building and managing your energy.

   a. Eat light and right; exercise daily (even if it's just a long walk); and get adequate rest.

---

[6] Note: This is not without some pain as you drill down into the crisis in detail. But it is totally worth it as the swirling thoughts in your head begin to subside and you get some cognitive distance from the situation so you can file it away for periods of time and get some sleep.

b. As you lay down to sleep each evening, make a 1-minute mental list of everything and everyone you are grateful for. This will provide perspective and put the crisis in its place.

c. Turn the crisis into a positive story—you can't change what happened, but you can choose the meaning you give to it.

d. Ask for help. No matter who you are, there is someone who will listen and help. We all face crises better as a team with wingmen.

The lessons you learn will be new arrows in your quiver for the next crisis. Thankfully, unlike my friends and others who have faced much tougher crises—heart attacks, aircraft crashes, cancer, addiction, loss of a child or spouse—it was a trial-run for bigger challenges ahead. I tried to see it as a training opportunity. I developed rituals and habits to keep me on top of my game physically, mentally, emotionally, and spiritually despite my anxieties and fears. It could have been a long, hard battle. My goal was to learn to live with it and how to compartmentalize so I could put my attention on other important matters. In the end, the crisis was resolved, and I emerged from the storm with a few scars. But I also became wiser and more confident in handling future storms.

Ultimately, the goal is to make the storm work for us rather than against us. Use it to make you stronger and more confident rather than weaker and more fearful.

Be a HIGH-TRUST Leader:
Build TRUST by building CHARACTER to walk your talk.

CHAPTER 5
COMMITMENT

Will you be with us when the going gets rough and play to win?

THE POWER OF PURPOSE

When I joined the Blue Angels as their flight leader, my teammates were absolutely certain I'd come to work with a smile on my face when the sun was shining, the sky was blue, and the air was smooth. But they also knew that we would encounter some storms, both figuratively and literally. And what they wanted to know was, "Will you be with us when the going gets rough?" And not only would I show up, but would I share in the struggle, sacrifice alongside them, and bring my A-game to lead our team safely through the storm? Would I play to win? Because if I was just showing up to take names, cast blame, point fingers, and CYA, forget about it!

Where does commitment come from? Why do some leaders have huge hearts that allow them to overcome tremendous adversity and setbacks? What causes people to persevere through challenges and failures, and keep coming back? I believe it comes from a very deep, very clear, and very intense sense of purpose. In the military, we called it "mission." When people know what mission they're on and why it is important, they can get up off the mat when they get knocked down. That's also what inspires them to go above and beyond what's required. When a leader helps their team get a clear idea of their mission and how serving together will help them get there, the leader doesn't have to motivate the team. They simply need to provide the necessary resources, training, and guidance, and then get out of their way because they will be souls on fire.

When the Blue Angels C-130 "Fat Albert" landed at an airport for the airshow each weekend, taxied up to the terminal, shut down its four engines, and hoisted the American flag, something special was about to happen. Out of that plane came the heart and soul of the Blue Angels: 45 of the most impressive young men and women I've ever met. Each one was devoted to the Team's mission and owned their important roles in its success. They immediately began preparing for the arrival of the six demonstration jets. Their motto was "The jets come first," and they would move mountains to ensure the jets were ready to fly each day. They took extraordinary pride in the fact that a Blue Angels airshow has never been canceled for maintenance issues since the team was formed in 1946.

In my experience, I've found that leaders are good at talking about "How" and "What." "Here's what we're going to do," and "Here's how we're going to do it." But these same leaders are reluctant to talk about the "Why." "Here's why we're doing this…" And teams are hungry for the "Why." They want to know why this work is important and why it's important to you as their leader. Only "Why" will capture their hearts and minds.

As Blue Angels, we could see our "why" every weekend in the smiles and enthusiasm of the people we met in cities and towns all across America. Visiting schools to inspire students to seek excellence and consider military service, visiting hospitals to brighten the day for patients, and spending time with our Navy and Marine colleagues when performing at military bases all kept us in touch with our mission.

DEMONSTRATING COMMITMENT

As the Blue Angels Flight Leader, I realized very quickly—as ALL leaders should recognize—I could have a good day and our team might have an average day, but our team could never have a great day if I didn't have a great day.

Early in the season we were doing an air show in El Paso, Texas. The wind was blowing 24 knots that day, gusting to 30–32, over a ridgeline west of the airport and creating significant turbulence over the airport. As we gathered for our preflight briefing, my wingmen looked somber and anxious. We discussed the situation, gathered input from everyone, adjusted a couple of the formations to provide an extra margin of safety, and agreed to give it a try. If anyone—in the air or on the ground— wasn't confident we could operate safely, we'd suspend the demonstration and land.

As we marched down, climbed in the jets, and taxied out in formation, I wasn't sure how the flight was going to go. I had flown in lots of bad weather, but never a Blue Angels airshow in that amount of turbulence.

As the Diamond (jets #1–#4) came to a stop on the runway, our maintenance officer, LT Clark "MO" Merritt announced on the radio,

"Boss, we own the airfield and the airspace. The winds are 260 at 24 gusting to 32, you're cleared for takeoff."

I acknowledged, "Thanks, MO!", took a deep breath, and announced our takeoff maneuver, "We're cleared for takeoff. Maneuver: Diamond Burner Loop with a left turnout."

The wingmen responded in order with their callsigns to confirm they heard me and understood, "Kato!" "Gucci!" "Scooter!"

Scooter (#4) called for the Diamond to switch to channel 16 on the radio, "Diamond half-clear on 16."

Me: "Let's run 'em up!"

We smoothly advanced the throttles to 85% power with our feet firmly on the brake pedals to keep from rolling; checked our engine instruments, and "wiped out the cockpit" by cycling the control stick to confirm proper operation of the flight controls. I looked to my left and Gucci gave me a thumbs up, indicating that he was ready. I looked to my right. On the right edge of the runway, Scooter gave Kato a thumbs up, which he then passed to me.

I looked down the runway and announced, "Smoke on!"

We each flicked a switch on our right throttle to activate a thin spray of oil into the right engine's exhaust to cause an eruption of white smoke behind the jets, announcing the Diamond's departure.

"Off brakes now!"

We lifted our feet off our brake pedals and the four jets lurched forward to begin our takeoff roll.

"Burners ready now!" When I said "now!", we simultaneously advanced our throttles full forward, and the jets surged as the eight General Electric F404 afterburners lit off.

As the jets accelerated, I concentrated on tracking my jet precisely straight down the runway. At 135 knots the jets reached flying speed and began to lift off the runway. Scooter was the last to get airborne, and when he called "Gear!", we raised the landing gear handle in our cockpits. At an altitude of 50 feet, I called, "A little drive", and pushed slightly forward on the stick to level the formation just above the runway. Behind me, Scooter applied full left rudder to slide his jet (wings level) under Kato's jet as the landing gear retracted. He took the slot position directly behind my jet's tailpipes as the acceleration increased.

At precisely 250 knots, I called "Up we go!"

On the "g" in "go," we smoothly pulled back on our control sticks and the formation climbed into the vertical at almost three times the force of gravity. I immediately felt the turbulence thumping my jet. I settled into my seat, my right hand firmly gripping the control stick and my forearm locked-in, resting on my thigh, to fly as stable of a profile as I could. I kept reminding myself to not react to the bumps and thumps of the wind, so the wingmen could safely stay in position a few feet from my jet.

As we came over the top of the loop, I tilted my head back to pick up the opposite horizon and called to reduce power and extend the speedbrakes to control our speed down the backside. Looking down at the runway, I called "Comes the pull", and we pulled back on our control sticks to finish the loop as the g-force pushed us down into our seats. We completed the maneuver by turning behind the crowd as Doc (#5) conducted his takeoff maneuver with an aileron roll with his landing gear extended. Yogi (#6) followed with a very low transition: raising his landing gear while keeping his jet only several feet off the runway. At the end of the runway, he violently pitched the aircraft straight up, climbed, and then pitched back to complete his Half-Cuban 8 maneuver in front of the crowd.

We flew in the turbulence with mind-numbing concentration. As the wingmen acknowledged my radio calls with their callsigns, I could tell they were working very hard but staying positive. Likewise, I ensured the tone of my voice was confident and positive. Halfway through the demo, as we continued to get bounced around, I couldn't resist sneaking a look in my rearview mirrors. All I saw behind me was blue and gold metal. Kato, Gucci, and Scooter were locked-in their positions, "Blue Angel close." Their determination and dedication to our mission was inspiring. The same was true for Doc and Yogi when they joined us for the final 6-plane Delta Formation maneuvers.

Despite very challenging conditions, we flew a safe, solid show that day. The large crowd on the ground had no idea how hard we were working. After all six jets landed, we taxied back to the flight line in formation. Once parked side-by-side in front of the crowd, we shut down our engines and raised our canopies in unison, unstrapped from our ejection seats, dismounted, and marched back just beyond my jet before concluding the demonstration with a sharp salute to the crowd. Amid the crowd's cheers and applause, we exchanged handshakes, high-fives, with large smiles of relief.

We were a different team after that show. That day my wingmen learned that even on the toughest day they could count on me to fly to the best of my ability. And I learned that on the toughest days they were going to enthusiastically support me and each other. After that show, we went to a new level of performance because our team climbed to a higher level of trust.

YOU GO FIRST

It's as simple and as challenging as that.

You call on your team to take new ground, to go somewhere new. And the team thinks, "Ok, you go first." Why? Because they want you to show them you mean it, that you are as committed to the mission as you are asking them to be.

Being a HIGH-TRUST Leader is not a safe place to be. But when the team sees you take the first bite, assume the same risks, and make the same sacrifices, they will join up despite any doubts or fears they may have.

HIGH-TRUST leaders are on a mission, and it is the mission and purpose that ignites and sustains their energy.

Build a clear, deep, and intense purpose and watch your commitment grow. Pretty soon you'll earn the reputation of having a "big heart" with huge resiliency. When the next storm hits, people will gravitate towards you because you have staying power.

IT'S NOT ABOUT YOU

HIGH-TRUST military leaders realize it is not about them, it's about the mission.

Many people aren't aware that each U.S. service member swears an oath upon entering the Navy, Marine Corps, Army, or Air Force (and periodically thereafter).

Many more people are not aware of the object of each Sailor's, Soldier's, Marine's, and Airman's "true faith and allegiance"—from the most senior general and admiral to the most junior seaman recruit, airman basic, and private. They don't swear allegiance to the President or the Secretary of Defense or the Chairman of the Joint Chiefs of Staff or any other person. They promise to "support and defend the Constitution of the United States against all enemies." That's the unifying strategic mission for all members of the Department of Defense reflected in the National Security Strategy. At each subsequent level, there are cascading, aligned operational missions for Navy fleets and USMC divisions within each geostrategic theater, and tactical missions for the naval strike groups with their air wings, ships, and submarines, and USMC regiments, battalions, and companies.

The amount of loyalty and trust given to each leader at every level is a direct function of their selfless commitment to the shared mission. When leaders demand, expect, or try to coerce trust and loyalty to themselves without a shared devotion to a higher calling, there is always friction, wariness, scorekeeping, and mistrust. But when the team believes the leader is fully committed to a common cause greater than himself or herself and is making shared sacrifices to serve the mission, the team will generously give their leader the gift of their trust and loyalty.

What is your team's mission? Or is your focus all about you and your success?

Do you clearly articulate it regularly, so all understand it and don't forget?

Have you (at least figuratively) sworn an oath to the mission? Or is your mission just a nice series of words in an email, a memo, a speech, or posted on your website? If you fake this, your actions—usually measured by your unwillingness to match the sacrifices you expect of your team— will invariably give you away, and the consequence will be lower trust and loyalty.

COMMITMENT TRAINING

Exercise #1: Clarify Your Purpose and Mission

1. Set aside an hour to reflect on and write about your purpose.

- Why is the work you do every day so important to you?

- Why is this relationship important?

- Why does it matter?[7]

- Transfer it to an index card and carry it with you. Read it aloud at least once a day this week

- Keep refining it. Make it more concise and truer. You'll know you're getting close when the hair begins to stand up on your neck when you hear your voice reading the words aloud. Record it on your iPhone and play it in the car on your way to or from work. Does it get you started on the right foot or energize you at the end of a tough day?

- Share your "Why" with others who matter to you. Watch their eyes light up when they hear your voice and feel your passion. Everyone wants to be on a hero's journey. When they realize you're on your way, maybe they'll mount-up on their own journey!

2. Build commitment by communicating a noble purpose that you truly believe.

---

[7] Don't rush this. Take time to get to the real "Why" and write it down as clearly as you can. What does it look like, feel like, smell like? You won't get it completely right in an hour, but if you're not distracted or interrupted, you'll get close.

- Make it inspiring and aspirational. This takes time and effort, but is worth it in spades. It is the fire that energizes the team and the key to resilience when a storm hits.

- Keep it alive every day through your actions and your example. The team won't believe in it any more than you do.

- Make it a key consideration in every decision. Is this decision consistent with our purpose and values? In military parlance, purpose is your team's strategic center of gravity.

- What are your measures for success?

- Are your weekly and daily priorities centered on a mission or is your attention diffused by whatever stuff keeps showing up in your inbox?

- Do your teammates share your vision because you took the time to share it with them? Not just the "What" and the "How," but more importantly, the "Why."

A while back, I led a leadership session with executives from a large insurance company. They struggled to verbalize their mission. They had no problem coming up with the usual corporate words to put on the wall, but nothing seemed to click or to energize them. Then someone mentioned Hurricane Katrina and faces lit up as they recalled deploying to New Orleans to help people rebuild their lives. It was a vivid experience that still evoked strong emotions, even tears. Suddenly, they connected with the deeper purpose of their work and a mission statement that fueled their passion: "We help people on their worst day."

How can you expect to accomplish great things—however you define them—if you are not clear about your purpose?

How will you avoid compromising and settling for less if your mission statement is antiseptic, meaningless, and gathering dust on a shelf?

Commitment Training Exercise #2: Demonstrate Your Commitment

1. Pick two important people in your life: one at work and one in your personal life.

2. Identify something they are each working on: a project, a goal, a problem, a cause.

3. Visit with each one this week and ask how it's going. Listen to the answer, ask questions to learn more. Don't give advice, offer solutions, or share your experiences. Just listen and learn. Often that is enough. If they want your advice, they'll ask for it.

4. Ask "Is there any way I can help?" If they provide an opportunity to help, do what you can without expectation of return.

Your actions will demonstrate your commitment to the relationship.

Be a HIGH-TRUST Leader:

Clarify your purpose to ignite your energy and prioritize your mission. Generously show up for those who matter to you.

CHAPTER 6
COMPETENCE

Are you skilled and relevant?

People often view competence as the most important criteria when making a trust decision, such as hiring, promotion, or a project assignment. What training and education has the individual completed? What experience do they have? What have they accomplished?

Competence is critical. But I intentionally place it third, because if the person doesn't have character and commitment, competence isn't that important. Sometimes referred to as "the tyranny of the expert," this individual may be wildly competent, but they are disruptive, creating a toxic work environment that negatively affects the team and its performance.

Each day, as we gathered in the conference room for our preflight briefing, I could see the third series of questions in my wingmen's eyes: "Are you good enough to be our leader today? Are you better than you were yesterday, but not as good as you'll be tomorrow? We don't want to stay here; we want to keep getting better, and we need our leader to keep improving every day."

In addition to being skilled, the individual's skills must be relevant for the mission. My wingmen were only mildly interested in my accomplishments as a dogfighter in air-to-air combat and as an accurate bomber who routinely received high grades during landing competitions on aircraft carriers. In truth, they only cared about my ability to fly airshows to Blue Angels' standards, day-after-day throughout the year.

To succeed as their leader required constant improvement; always accepting the discomfort of pushing the boundaries of my performance; always willing to accept positive constructive feedback every day in order to get better and better and better.

THE FOUR STAGES OF COMPETENCE[8]

Below are the four stages of competence as illustrated by my progress to master the skills necessary to lead a Blue Angels flight demonstration:

1. **Unconscious Incompetence.** Watching airshows over the years and seeing the team up close during the last month of the previous season, I knew I had a lot to learn, but there was still so much I didn't realize. One skill was talking on the radios while flying. Navy and Marine aviators take pride in minimal transmissions on the radios—crisp, precise, and limited to avoiding garbling the radio frequency with unnecessary chatter. In Blue Angels flying, the jets are so close together that the leader must transmit a cadence of commands on the radio

---

[8] From *Management of Training Programs*, 1960, by Frank A. DePhillips, Wiliam M. Berliner, and James J. Cribbin.

so that all six pilots can safely fly their jets in unison. So, not only did I have to fly the jet precisely, but I also had to learn to make the correct radio calls before moving the control stick or the throttles from the moment we taxied until the engines were shut down when parked after the flight.

2. **Conscious Incompetence.** During my first flight with Kato (#2), it quickly became clear I had a long way to go to talk and fly even the basic maneuvers with enough precision and consistency so the wingmen could ultimately fly within a couple of feet of my jet while we looped and rolled at high speeds and very low altitudes. I had a long way to go to earn HIGH-TRUST.

3. **Conscious Competence.** This is when I achieved the knowledge and skills to successfully lead a Blue Angels flight demonstration. My challenge at this stage was to remain consciously aware of all the procedures and techniques (similar to RAM memory in a computer). I had all the procedures and numbers in my head, but any significant distraction or letting my mind wander or fixate could jeopardize my concentration and performance. I achieved this near the completion of Winter Training as we began the airshow season.

4. **Unconscious Competence.** This is the goal, and it didn't occur until about halfway through my first airshow season. At that point, I had flown enough practice flights and airshows at various locations that the procedures, muscle memory, techniques, radio calls, and visual scan were now hardwired as habits in my subconscious. I'm no longer climbing in the jet, I'm strapping it on with the bandwidth to factor in the local terrain, the winds, the clouds, and other conditions. The show became an artistry of power, agility, and precision rather than

rote maneuvers. I was now unconsciously competent. This is where the exhilaration of being in "the zone" or achieving "flow" resides. But this is not a "set it and forget it" condition. It took continual daily effort to retain mastery and avoid the slippery slope of complacency and losing my edge.

LEARNER'S MINDSET

Achieving unconscious competence requires a dedication to daily improvement and serves someone well until the environment, the mission, the technology, or the competition changes. Then, one must become a beginner again to regain relevance and do the work to climb back to unconscious competence.

During my second Winter Training, I went back to basics and focused on the fundamentals with three new wingmen as we rebuilt the team for the new season. After my tour was complete and I transferred to become Deputy Commander, Carrier Air Wing Seven, I was back in the Navy's tactical fleet environment, where I was faced with changes in hardware, software, and tactics over the past 30 months. I had to assume a learner's mindset again and step through the four stages of competence to become a HIGH-TRUST leader of the air wing.

Once you achieve the mastery of unconscious competence, life is good. You are on your game; you have opened the window to mastery. People view you as a special talent in your field. But then something inevitably changes. It can be rapid (boom!) or slowly over time (drip, drip, drip). The change can originate in the external environment (i.e., changes in the market, new competitors, new technology) or it can be an internal change in your role (or strategy, product, services, priorities, etc.). Even if they are unconsciously competent, skilled leaders can quickly become less and less relevant if they don't adapt to changes.

But how do they adapt? They must go back down to a state of unconscious or conscious incompetence and work their way back up to mastery in the new environment by developing new skills. It's not easy. Especially when you've been regarded as the ace-of-the-base by your teammates, your boss, your family, your friends, and your competitors. It can be a source of self-denial and a huge resistance to change.

In my current world of flying corporate jets, I know outstanding older pilots who have been flying a particular model aircraft for many years (e.g., "I'm a Gulfstream guy."). And then one day, the company or owner considers purchasing a new jet from a different manufacturer. I've seen long-time professional pilots panic at the thought of having to learn a new aircraft with different systems, performance characteristics, and a different network of technical support. Their ego can't handle the discomfort of being a beginner again (albeit a beginner with lots of experience).

Are you resisting what is required for you to stay relevant in your world? Being a beginner again is awkward and humbling. Our precious egos hate the thought. Let me ask you one question that will help illuminate to what degree you have a learner's mindset:

When was the last time you did something for the first time?

PERFECT PRACTICE

Growing up, we often heard a common saying from parents, coaches, and teachers that "Practice makes perfect." Our Blue Angels team didn't believe that adage. We believed practice made consistency. Practicing poorly, haphazardly, indifferently, or infrequently would result in poor performance. Applying Anders Ericsson's description of "deliberate practice" in his book, *Peak*, our saying was, "Perfect practice makes perfect." We never sauntered out to the jets and straggled out to the runway for takeoff. Every practice flight was focused and deliberate:

- We would line up and follow our standard procedures from beginning to end.

- Our training flights were organized to focus on specific portions of the flight demonstration that needed improvement or refreshment.

- Before every flight, be it practice or airshow, each pilot would identify a very specific goal to improve their performance.

- Our motto was, "Practice 'til we get it right and keep practicing until we can't get it wrong."

This disciplined attitude of perfect practice was a critical contributor to preserving safety while flying at the limits of human capability every day. The four elements of our perfect practice were:

1. Embrace a learner's mindset; be humble; check your ego at the door; accept mistakes as part of the process; be patient; don't get discouraged.

2. Practice outside your comfort zone; focus on challenging gaps in performance; keep raising the bar.

3. Be consistent; not just now and then, but every time, always.

4. Seek and welcome feedback; engage in a candid, constructive, thorough debrief after every flight.

THE DEBRIEF

We debriefed after every flight, period. Not now and then. Not as an afterthought. Not only if it fit into everyone's schedule. No excused absences. Every flight had a debrief: during pre-season training, mid-week practice, and after airshows. Everything else could wait or be rescheduled. Actually, there was one flight each year that we didn't conduct a formal debrief. It was on the last day of the season at our Homecoming Airshow at NAS Pensacola. We didn't debrief because that team would never fly together again (although each of us informally looked at the videotape. We couldn't help ourselves; it had become a habit.)

Each debrief would start promptly on time, with rank and egos left at the door. Only the current team and any former or honorary Blue Angels who happened to be in town were allowed in the room. No friends, family, or curious guests. We wanted complete candor and trust with no distractions as we reviewed and analyzed our performance. The debrief was divided into three parts: General and Safe, Detailed Review/Analysis, and Conclusion. It included not only the F/A-18 and C-130 pilots, but all the support officers who had specific roles and responsibilities in the control tower, at the communications cart, and on the speaker's stand for the narration.

GENERAL AND SAFE

The purpose of the General and Safe portion is to address any big-picture items or safety issues during the flight. General items could be something that caused a delay in the airshow schedule, a maintenance problem with one of the jets, an issue with the local FAA rep, a problem with the placement of the centerpoint marker, etc. Safe items would be anything that anyone observed that was a safety concern.

General. I would start the debrief with a couple of brief general comments about our portion of the airshow and solicit input and discussion from everyone else.

Safe. As the flight leader, I would then set the example by listing any significant mistakes I made that could have jeopardized the safety of the flight. Then, I would call on each of the other jet pilots, the C-130 pilots, and the support officers to do the same. This portion of the debrief was critical for a few reasons:

1. The purpose of the debrief is learning. If someone had a close call or made a mistake that caused a "significant emotional event," no learning was going to occur until we addressed and resolved the issue. This typically included taking responsibility for the event, identifying what action(s) was needed to prevent it from happening again, and committing to avoid a recurrence in the future. Only then could we move on to learning.

2. The payoff for giving each person a chance to admit their mistakes was two-fold:

   a. If someone was making a mistake and wasn't aware of it or the implications it had on others, we needed to make them aware of it.

   b. If someone was making a mistake and wouldn't admit it, we had another problem to discuss.

As the leader, it was my responsibility to set the example that mistakes were part of learning and continuous improvement. Mistakes were expected, as long as they weren't the result of negligence in preparation or execution. Each of us was expected to own our performance and accept daily feedback without getting defensive or discouraged.

DETAILED REVIEW AND ANALYSIS

Our Flight Surgeon, LT Bryan "Buckwitch" Buchanan, was the expert observer for the demonstration. During Winter Training, he and our

Aircraft Maintenance Officer, LT Clark "MO" Merritt, spent every flight at CenterPoint in the desert or at the airfield to refine their eyes and the nuances of each maneuver. During the detailed debrief, Buckwitch would announce the placement of the maneuver in relation to CenterPoint (a visible marker such as a tractor trailer, white bus, or Coast Guard boat at the middle of the showline), any deviation in the formation or altitude, and how the maneuver looked to the crowd.

C-130 Debrief: Buckwitch would step through each of Fat Albert's maneuvers one-by-one and the pilot in command (PIC) would play the video tape and discuss them with his co-pilot. Anyone else who had a question or comment could contribute.

Jet Demo Debrief: We would step through the entire demonstration—from marching to the jets until the final hand salute—with Buckwitch sharing his critique followed by a review of the videotape and detailed discussion. Scooter (#4) ran the video replay for the Diamond (4 jets) and Delta (6 jets) maneuvers and Doc (#5) for the Solos (2 jets) maneuvers. Each of us would evaluate our performance and comment on the specific goal we each set for that flight.

GETTING NAKED IN THE DEBRIEF

The Blue Angels ethos includes absolute candor during postflight debriefs. Rank is figuratively removed upon entering the room as everyone is viewed as equally valued in assessing our performance. When the stakes and consequences are so high, there can be no impediment to objectively assessing the whole truth of our performance with 100% commitment by everyone to improve our performance every day. I called this unique level of candor "getting naked" in the debrief.

If I was making a mistake and didn't realize it, I wasn't going to avoid doing it again. If I was making a mistake and not willing to admit it, I wasn't going to improve. Who wants to follow someone who is unaware or unwilling to admit when they're wrong?

My most memorable debrief occurred during the first week of Winter Training in El Centro, CA. It was initially very painful due to lots of frustration, emotion, and fatigue. But it radically changed my mindset, and it was the key to my success over the next two years. The shared vulnerability was the basis for the enduring friendships with my teammates for the rest of my life.

Measured against the Blue Angel standard, the first flight that day was a mixture of good and not so good. The maneuvers we had been practicing were coming along fine, but the newer ones were a bit rough. I hadn't flown enough repetitions ("reps") to get them grooved into "conscious competence."[9] Although I was expected to be able to recount every flaw in my performance during the debrief, frankly, my memory bucket was full after the 3rd or 4th maneuver. In the debrief, Scooter (#4) stepped us through the flight from beginning to end. When my memory became sporadic, Scooter and Kato (#2) filled in what they observed. When you're flying that close together, your wingmen don't miss any deviations from the prescribed profile of each maneuver. It had been a long, tiring week of 2–3 flights per day, trying to be perfect while keeping all the procedures in my head, making mistakes, and recounting them one by one in the debriefs. The combination of frustration and fatigue got the better of me. At one point, I looked at Kato and Scooter and blurted defensively, "C'mon you guys, can't you see I'm trying as hard as I can here?!"

---

[9] To revisit the concept of "Conscious Competence." flip back to page 75.

Thankfully, they didn't respond in kind to my emotion. As a pair, Kato and Scooter had different temperaments that perfectly complemented each other in their roles as coaches for Gucci (#3) and me during our first year as Blue Angels. Always professional and objective, never personal, they showed no frustration or impatience. Kato was a disciplined, by-the-book, methodical Marine who left no stone unturned. Scooter's manner was encouraging and nurturing, but no less demanding. In response to my outburst, they glanced at each other, and Kato calmly said, "Roger that, Boss, we know you're trying hard, but we don't grade on effort, we go by performance, and these maneuvers aren't cutting it. We've got a long way to go." Scooter followed up with a little encouragement, "That's right, Boss, you have too much wing movement, and we can't fly as close to you as we need to. Hang in there, keep working, and we'll get there."

At that moment, I looked around the table with my bruised ego after a long week and instead of seeing critics, I saw loyal teammates who earnestly wanted me to succeed. They weren't trying to make me look bad or playing any head games. They were giving me the precious gift of a mirror to view my performance. No rationalization, no excuses. A gift to help me improve and succeed because our performance as a team would never be any better than my performance as the leader.

My job was to fly the maneuvers as consistently and smoothly as possible, placing each one precisely over CenterPoint, so the wingmen could show the world what superb aviators they were. When I recognized that Kato and Scooter were 100% dedicated to helping me become the best flight leader I could be, my attitude towards their feedback changed and my performance significantly improved.

The candid debriefs (and the many that followed), the shared vulnerability of flying "Blue Angel close" throughout the season, and the entire squadron striving together to set the bar as high as possible forged deep and lasting friendships grounded in the highest level of trust and camaraderie that has never faded. It was magical.

THOUGHTS ON FEEDBACK

- Feedback is a GIFT. It is essential to learning and mastery.

- Each individual is responsible for delivering feedback in a candid, constructive manner.

- Each individual is responsible for their response to feedback. Keep your ego in check.

- Listen to understand the feedback; don't defend, deny, destroy.

- Many people have trouble accepting positive feedback. Don't discount it; double-down and reinforce what is working.

- People who don't like us often give us the most honest feedback. Despite how the message is delivered, objectively evaluate it to see if there are any valuable insights. If there are none, discard it.

- Be wary of mixing positive and negative feedback. Often, a negative comment will overshadow a positive one. Conversely, if we're not clear and direct (with respect) about highlighting deficiencies in performance, the message may not get through.

DEBRIEFING GUIDELINES AND NORMS

1. Just do it. Regularly. You'll get better at it with practice.

2. Make it a habit. There are a thousand excuses not to have one; none outweigh its value.

3. Schedule it during the planning process, not as an afterthought.

4. The leader ensures a safe environment and sets the example.

5. Objectively evaluate your own performance first.

6. Everyone participates and accepts responsibility for their performance.

7. Honesty isn't enough; candor and vulnerability are expected.

8. Defuse emotions and egos with positive intentions.

9. Ask questions to uncover a deeper understanding.

10. Ask each other, "What happened?" "Why did it happen?" "How can we apply these lessons and share them with others?"

11. Show appreciation for the gift of feedback to help you improve.

12. You know your team has the right attitude when someone confesses to making a mistake that no one else would have noticed. They do this to help their teammates avoid making the same mistake.

CONCLUSION AND "I'M GLAD TO BE HERE."

To conclude the debrief, we'd give everyone a chance to make any final comments. I would start by making some overall remarks and briefly recapping the lessons I learned to apply to the next flight. I would then call on each of the officers and any former or honorary Blue Angels for their thoughts. We would each end our remarks with the same five words to remind ourselves and everyone else what a privilege it was to be part of such a special organization. We would simply say, "I'm glad to be here."

"I'm glad to be here." Such a simple ritual. Often thought to be too corny for highly accomplished people. Hardly worth noticing in a world of cynicism. Except that it has power. When you've had a bad day or stress and fatigue are causing feelings of frustration or dejection, saying those words out loud can reframe your attitude and perspective. And hearing all our teammates say those words caused positive feelings that were contagious.

COMPETENCE TRAINING

Training Exercise #1: Debrief Your Own Performance

1. Pick one small goal for improvement this week. Don't make it radical: just one area you've noticed could use your attention to raise your game.

2. Write it down. Be very specific.

3. Accept responsibility each day to get a little better. "Today I will _____."

4. Reflect on your performance in a 5-minute daily written debrief.

5. Evaluate your progress at the end of the week and reward yourself accordingly.

6. Rinse and repeat the next week.

Training Exercise #2: Make Debriefing a Habit on Your Team

- Schedule a mandatory debrief when planning your next project or event.

- Let everyone know how the debrief will be conducted and what information you expect them to bring.

- Conduct the debrief as scheduled, shortly after the event or project.

- Follow the debriefing guidelines listed above.

- The first time is the worst. Each debrief will get better with practice.

Be a HIGH-TRUST Leader:

Build and sustain competence through perfect practice, feedback, and continuous learning.

CHAPTER 7
CONNECTION

Do they believe I understand them?

By July, we hit mid-season form. As I described earlier, I could literally change the trajectory of a maneuver based on the inflection of my voice on the radio—not the words, but how I said the words! If I needed to speed the formation's rate of roll to keep us underneath the clouds, pull more G's at the bottom of a loop to stay above a ridge line, or turn the formation sharper to navigate around a skyscraper, my wingmen would stay with me because they knew I understood what I was asking them to do. But if one of them doubted I was taking their situation into consideration when making a decision, there would be hesitation and possibly increased separation and distraction due to lower trust.

The question I asked myself was, "Do they believe I understand them?" Notice it is a different question than, "Do I believe I understand them?" What I think may have been interesting to me, but it was not sufficient.

What mattered was, "What do they believe?" When they believed that I "got them," that I understood their situation and challenges, their hopes and concerns, and that I was open to their ideas and recommendations, they would stay with me without hesitation.

Making connections is the pillar of trust many high-speed leaders are missing because they are moving at Mach 2, seeking to be as efficient as possible in everything they do. The problem is, you can be efficient with things, but you can't be efficient with people. To make connections requires slowing down and taking the time to listen and understand others. This is something many leaders miss. And it costs them more than they realize.

Why? Because we don't see the world as it is, we see it as we are. Everyone sees the world and events in their own way, from their own perspective and life experience. No two of us see life exactly the same. A HIGH-TRUST Leader must be able to see the world through their teammates' eyes, stepping away from his or her window to look through theirs from time to time.

Why? Because teammates, direct reports, colleagues, clients, customers, bosses, spouses, and teenage children are asking themselves every day in some form or fashion, "Does she (or he) understand me?"

Listening is the essential skill for establishing meaningful connections. Not listening with the little voice in my head that prepares to defend, deny, discount, or persuade. But listening with full attention and curiosity to understand how the other person sees and feels about the situation, the task, the goal, the mission. I found that my teammates didn't need to get their way all the time, but they did need to feel heard and understood. Without connection, there's always hesitancy, disengagement, and lower trust.

The biggest barriers to connection are allocating time, an ability to listen empathically, and the willingness to give someone else our full attention. This is what my wife is referring to when she opens up about something that's bothering her. After a few minutes she stops, her eyes narrow, and she says, "You're not listening! You're waiting!" And she's right. She's sharing her feelings, seeking empathy, and I'm wired to solve her problem. After she's gotten a few sentences out, I have the answer, and now I'm just waiting for her to take a breath so I can announce the answer and we can move on! These days, she starts by saying, "I don't want you to fix this, I just want you to listen." I'm a work in progress, like everyone else.

We must slow down to connect with the people who matter to us. We must open our eyes, our ears, and our hearts to see the world through their eyes. During that time, we must put away our gizmos that make our lives so efficient but distract us from paying attention to others. If commitment is about winning their minds, connection is about winning their hearts. Remember, trust can't be demanded, expected, bought, or coerced. It is a gift that must be earned every day through the keyhole of CONNECTION. Diverse and virtual teams require extra effort to build connections. It's worth it.

Be a HIGH-TRUST Leader: step away from your window and view the world through theirs. Show you understand them and watch their trust grow.

BARRIERS TO CONNECTION

There are many barriers to connection that must be overcome:

- Impatience: I don't have time to listen carefully. Just get to the bottom line.

- Insecurity: I'm afraid that if I really listen, they will persuade me and get their way, they will win.

- Needing to persuade: I'm not here to listen or understand, I must get you to agree with me.

- Indifference: I don't really care what you think or feel, or what challenges you face.

- Ego: This relationship is about me; I don't need to understand you, your role is to understand me; I'm the boss, the client, the parent, etc.

- Quick to conclude: Here we go again, I don't need to listen because I've seen this many times, I already know all I need to know.

- Miscommunication: I don't understand your language, your context, or what you mean, but I'll assume I do.

- Prejudice: I don't need to listen, I already know about your "kind," your culture, your generation.

- Distraction: You're not important enough to me to deserve my full attention. I can listen while I text, look around the room, listen to music, check incoming emails, etc.

- Interruption: That's enough, now let me tell you what I think, what I've done, etc.

Truly making a connection so that someone feels deeply understood requires the opposite of all the barriers above. Mostly it takes time, curiosity, and a caring heart.

BUILDING CONNECTION

The Blue Angels have a rule that they take off their sunglasses when meeting with the public after flying an airshow or having their picture taken. It's a little thing, but has a big effect. They want to connect eye-to-eye with whomever they are speaking to; to inspire young and old alike. 15 years after flying with the Team, I received an email from a father from Tucson, AZ where we had flown our second airshow that season. He reminded me that I had spoken to him and his six-year-old son at the crowdline after the show. He said he was writing to let me know that his son was soon to graduate from the U.S. Naval Academy, heading to flight school to become a naval aviator, and his son credits our brief visit as the spark that began his journey.

People don't care how much you know, what you know, who you are, or what you're selling until they know that you care enough about them to understand their concerns, their ideas, their goals, and their story.

How can you show how much you care?

- Learn their names, their stories, their interests, their children.
- Look them in the eye when you speak to them.
- Slow down and give them your full attention.
- Put away your phone. Don't keep glancing at your smartwatch.
- Let them talk.
- Reply to their emails; return their calls; acknowledge their texts.
- Ask for their opinion and truly listen to their answer.
- Show respect.

- Recognize their outstanding performance, effort, and sacrifice.

- Extend trust by delegating authority and responsibility.

- Make a personal sacrifice of your time and energy on their behalf.

You get the idea. This isn't rocket science. The impact and value of showing you care is far greater than the time and effort expended because it is rare and unexpected. Warning: don't try this if you don't mean it. The penalty for insincerity counts double.

IN DISAGREEMENTS, FOLLOW RAPOPORT'S RULES

It's easy to connect with someone you agree with. You are already in alignment. It's much harder to connect with someone who disagrees with you. How do you get them to believe you understand them?

In his book, *Intuition Pumps and Other Tools for Thinking*, Daniel Dennett shares a practical strategy for building connection and opening the window to persuasion. This strategy is derived from the work of Anatol Rapoport, a mathematical psychologist.

When having an argument with someone, follow these steps:

- Attempt to re-express the other person's position so clearly, vividly, and fairly that he says, "Thanks, I wish I'd thought of putting it that way."

- List any points of agreement, especially if they are not matters of general or widespread agreement.

- Mention anything new you learned from the other person's argument.

- Only then are you permitted to say so much as a word of rebuttal or criticism.

- Follow these steps and the other person will feel understood. And if your rebuttal is rational, reasonable, and supported with facts and/or examples, you might also change their mind. Wouldn't that be a refreshing outcome in our polarized culture?

People don't necessarily need to win the argument. But they do need to feel heard and understood if they are going to trust.

DO YOU NEED TO CHANGE YOUR STORY?

It is easy to seek connection to people we like, people like us, and people who have not disappointed us in the past. It's harder to seek connection to people who are different, who see the world differently, who have different interests, and especially people who have caused us pain.

For those people, we often have perceptions and stories that we tell ourselves over and over about them. Times may change, people may change, but we keep the same stories. Sometimes these stories get in the way and prevent us from making the effort to understand them, their perspective, and their motivations. We interpret their behaviors and assign intentions that may or may not be true. And that oft-repeated story prevents us from questioning our assumptions.

If the relationship is difficult, yet important, every now and then we need to clean the slate and reevaluate our story that describes their behavior. We need to ask open-ended questions to see the world from their perspective, the view from their window. And we need to be open to the possibility that the impediment to making a connection and building trust is not them—it is us and our faulty story.

CONNECTING UP

Positional leaders typically think of the importance of connecting with their direct reports, their peers, and their subordinates. But it is also very important to connect with your seniors.

When your boss truly believes that you understand him or her, trust goes up, and the conversation changes. Consider the alternative: if your boss doesn't believe you understand him or her, that you don't realize what they're trying to do and why, then there's wariness often followed by micromanagement and an absence of delegation and granting autonomy.

10 THINGS TO SAY TO BUILD CONNECTION

Below are 10 things you can say to help build CONNECTION so the other person—your boss, your teammate, your teenager, your spouse, your direct report—feels understood. When they feel understood, the window of TRUST begins to open.

"Here's what I'm thinking." Taking the time to explain your decisions opens those decisions up to discussion or criticism, it also opens up your decisions to improvement.

"I was wrong." When you're wrong, say you're wrong. You won't lose respect, you'll gain it.

"I was really impressed when you [fill in the specifics]." Specific, authentic praise is a gift that costs the giver nothing but is priceless to the recipient. Start praising. The people around you will love you for it. But the praise must be authentic and deserved. I have a colleague who praises everything and has lost credibility. It's just white noise.

"You're welcome." Think about a time you gave a gift and the recipient seemed uncomfortable, awkward, or didn't acknowledge it. Did their reaction take away a little of the fun for you? The same thing can happen when you are thanked. Don't spoil the moment or the fun for the other person. Make eye contact and say, "You're welcome. I was glad to do it." Avoid replying with "No problem." You may not realize it, but you're dismissing their appreciation.

"Can you help me?" When you need help, just say, sincerely and humbly, "Can you help me?" In the process you'll show vulnerability, respect, and a willingness to listen—all qualities of a great leader and a great friend.

"I'm sorry." We all make mistakes. Say you're sorry, say why you're sorry, and take all the blame. No less. No more. If you then show you're sorry by your behavior, you both get to make the freshest of fresh starts.

"Can you show me?" Advice is temporary; knowledge is forever. Knowing what to do helps, but knowing how or why to do it means everything. When you ask to be taught or shown, several things happen: you implicitly show you respect the person giving the advice; you show you trust his or her experience, skill, and insight; and you get to better assess the value of the advice. Don't just ask for input. Ask to be taught, trained, or shown—then you both win.

"Let me give you a hand." Many people see asking for help as a sign of weakness, or they don't ask because they "don't want to be a bother." So, many people hesitate to ask for help. But everyone needs help. Don't just say, "Is there anything I can help you with?" Most people will give you a version of the reflexive reply to salesclerks, "No, I'm just looking," or "No, I'm all right." Be specific. Find something you can help with. Say "I've got a few minutes. Can I help you finish that?" Offer in a way that feels collaborative, not patronizing or gratuitous. Model the behavior you want your teammates to display. Then actually roll up your sleeves and help.

"I love you." No, not at work, but everywhere else you mean it and every time you feel it.

Nothing. Sometimes the best thing to say is nothing. If you're upset, frustrated, or angry, stay quiet. You may think venting will make you feel better afterward, but it never does.

CONNECTION TRAINING

Training Exercise #1: Practice Listening to Understand.

The objective of this exercise is to practice listening without distraction, to ask open-ended questions, and to show you understand the other person.

1. Invite a teammate to go for a walk or to get coffee or lunch. Let them know your intention is to spend a few minutes together simply to get better acquainted.

2. Check your attitude. Put their interests before yours; summon your patience and curiosity.

3. Start them talking about something meaningful with open-ended questions, such as:

   • What was it like where you grew up?

   • What do you like to do when away from work?

- What are you known for among your friends?

- Describe what a really good day looks like.

4. Listen to their responses.

   - Just listen without interrupting, interpreting, or adding.

   - Ask questions to gain deeper understanding. "Tell me more…"

5. Confirmation cycle.

   A. State your understanding of what they shared, using some of their words.

   B. Allow them to correct you about something, even if you repeated what they shared word for word.

   C. Return to step A with your new understanding until they confirm that you get it (e.g., "Yes, that's right.").

Training Exercise #2: Practice Rapoport's Rules

In these polarized days, many people have gotten to the point where they shy away from any disagreement (e.g., "Too much negative emotion."). But what if you made the disagreement into a game with the objective to state their position better than they did?

- Detach your ego from your position on an issue and accept that honorable people can disagree.

- Invite a friend to meet for coffee who you know has a different opinion on an issue.

- Remind yourself that the goal is to practice Rapoport's rules, not necessarily to change their mind (although you might).

- During the conversation, practice the rules whenever you disagree.

- Repeat this exercise with various friends until you become comfortable with the rules.

- You are now prepared to build connection with anyone willing to have a meaningful, productive conversation.

Be a HIGH-TRUST Leader:
Build and maintain connection by investing time
and attention to help people feel understood.

CHAPTER 8
COMMUNICATION

Do they understand me?

C ommunication is the lubricant of the **HIGH-TRUST** engine. If connection means my teammates believe I understand them, good communication means they understand me.

It's difficult to trust someone you don't understand. When communication is lacking or ineffective in a dynamic relationship, trust is in jeopardy. When communication is poor, frustration increases, productivity decreases, more time is required to fix mistakes, drama has to be dealt with, and trust needs to be restored. At 500 mph, we didn't have time to deal with misunderstandings.

During a Blue Angel airshow, we were as precise with our communications as we were about our flying. As the leader, I made routine radio transmissions regarding where the formation was and what was coming next: "We're behind the crowd, setting up the Delta Roll maneuver." These messages provided awareness to the entire team and reassurance to the wingmen that all was OK, and the show was progressing as briefed. This allowed them to remain totally focused on the jet two feet away from them flying at nearly 400 mph. In fighter pilot lingo we called it "SA," or situational awareness. Without routine descriptive communication, the wingmen would wonder, "What's going on?" "Where are we?" "Is everything OK?" Doubts would grow into hesitation. They might sneak a peek at the ground below to see where we were. A momentary distraction could cause a mishap.

Prior to commencing any maneuver, I would confirm we had 2-way communication within the formation. I would announce the maneuver and the five wingmen would answer in numerical order with their callsigns or nicknames. If someone didn't answer, I'd repeat. If still no answer, I would call "No maneuver," and we'd spread out, climb away from the ground, and resolve the situation. If unable to restore communication, whoever could not transmit or receive would land and get in the 2-seat #7 jet and rejoin. Although this was a procedure we followed on every flight, it never happened during my two years on the Team.

Throughout aviation, a lot of training and effort is dedicated to developing effective communication. Misunderstandings can be deadly if a pilot misunderstands what altitude she is assigned, a tower controller uses non-standard terminology at a busy airport, or the crew of an airliner neglects to keep each other informed.

How can you trust someone who doesn't communicate effectively?

Every Blue Angel flight debrief addressed the team's communication and how it could be improved, both in the air and on the ground. Our goal was to make our communication so clear, concise, and direct that everyone understood the message the first time and the intended recipients had no doubt it was meant for them.

How often have you experienced a leader who neglects to communicate, whose message is muddled, or not clearly directed to the intended recipient? Think about the incredible amount of information bombarding us every day from all directions trying to capture our attention. Leaders must be very clear, concise, consistent, and direct to cut through the noise.

The biggest problem with communication for leaders is the presumption that it has occurred.

"I sent the email; he gets it."

"I gave the speech; they get it."

"I had a one-on-one meeting; she understands."

"I texted him; he knows."

They don't. At least not yet. How many times do you have to hear a new song before you understand the lyrics? Messages must be transmitted multiple times, in various ways, in a consistent manner until the recipients confirm they successfully received it.

In aviation, there are very specific procedures to ensure effective communication. A pilot is required to read back a route assignment or altitude clearance received from Air Traffic Control verbatim to confirm the clearance was accurately received and understood. Leaders need to adopt similar methods of confirmation to ensure the message received was what they intended.

THE STORIES WE ASSUME

Human beings are natural story-makers and storytellers. In the absence of communication, members of your team will develop their own stories about other people's intentions, assumptions, and behaviors. Over time, these stories can wildly diverge from the truth and cause significant gaps in relationships due to mistrust.

ESTABLISH A COMMUNICATION CADENCE

As described earlier, during a flight demonstration, my wingmen knew when they would hear from me on the radios. If one of us neglected to communicate when expected, it was a red flag that something out of the ordinary was happening and needed to be resolved.

A defined communication cadence ensures timely, regular interactions to establish and maintain mutual understanding and connection and helps to avoid gaps.

- Your team should know when they will next hear from you and when they'll get a chance to speak. This cuts down on drop-in questions and interruptions when they don't know when they'll hear from you.

- Transmit your candid assessment of the current situation and your intentions.

- By communicating regularly, your team avoids inaccurate stories, rumors, and gossip that build up over time. They get a chance to ask questions, report information, and make suggestions.

- If there is a gap in communication and gossip appears, give your teammates the benefit of the doubt until your impression can be confirmed or discarded.

- Seek to dispel unfounded criticisms of teammates and negativity based simply on assumptions. Ask, "Are you sure?" "How do you know?" "Have you discussed it with them?"

Everyone is responsible for keeping the communication paths open and flowing. If you need more, ask for it. If a teammate is a poor communicator, reach out to communicate and sustain trust.

THINK BEFORE YOU SPEAK

In aviation, pilots who speak calmly and coolly on the radios during emergencies or moments of high stress are highly respected. Their stable demeanor communicates great confidence and competence. The secret to sounding cool and calm is to think about what you want to say before you say it.

Everyone is painfully aware when someone is talking before thinking. Often, the talk is wasted because no one listened as the speaker rambled incoherently or mumbled their message. And if emotions are high, the message can be difficult to understand.

To be a better communicator, pay attention to this axiom. It's the only way your message will be concise. And if it's clear and concise, it might just be heard by the audience you are talking to, whether it be your colleague, your business team, or your teenager.

Years ago, I was asked to deliver a TEDx Talk on HIGH-TRUST Leadership in 12 minutes. Whew. My usual presentation was an hour or more, so I had to distill it down to its essence. It took me about six tries to get there. Each cut became more difficult. But when I finally got it right, it made my subsequent presentations so much better because I made the extra effort to get very clear about the core of my message.

COMMUNICATION TRUST KILLERS

Avoid the following if you want to maintain a HIGH-TRUST reputation:

- Excuses
- Gossip
- Complaining
- Interrupting
- Talking over others
- Passive aggression
- Reflexive negativity
- Distracted by smartphone
- Impatience
- Dismissive
- Rushing to judgment
- Stereotyping
- Defensiveness
- Exaggeration

Characteristics of HIGH-TRUST communication:

- Eye contact

- Curious, inquisitive, open to new ideas

- Truthful, honest, candid

- Willingness to be vulnerable

- Attentive

- Appreciative

- Patient

- Replay the message to convey understanding

- Honorable personal example

It's not a coincidence that the first list breeds mistrust and the second list enhances trustworthiness. Ask a truth-teller to make you aware when you fall into the trap of the first list. Compliment others when they speak in accordance with the second list.

DISPEL MISUNDERSTANDINGS

When trust is lacking, it is not uncommon to rush to judgment and not take time to confirm what the person really meant or what really happened. It is much easier to jump to conclusions, assume the worst, and spread unhappiness at the water cooler. Unfortunately, with 21st century social media, smartphones, email, and texts, the water cooler is now global in size, with near-instantaneous gossip spread to the multitudes. Asynchronous communication using hastily written texts, emails, and tweets can be radioactive, with a half-life lasting centuries.

It's best to confirm your source and take steps to avoid misunderstandings before making a judgment and breaking trust. Give others the benefit of doubt and take a moment to confirm what you think you know. If your worst suspicions turn out to be true, there will be time later to take remedial action. If your initial impression was wrong and you announced your anger, fear, disappointment to one and all, it will take lots of time and energy to put the genie back in the bottle. You may not be able to un-ring the bell. As the saying goes, an ounce of prevention is cheaper than a pound of cure.

PROMOTE CANDOR

An agile, dynamic HIGH-TRUST team requires much more than honesty. It requires candor. Candor is the willingness to speak the truth as you understand it *without being prompted*.

During a Blue Angels airshow, we were moving so fast that if I had to ask to get the truth it would be too late. I needed people to bring me the truth when I needed to hear it. I needed candor.

At the Navy Fighter Weapons School ("TOPGUN") and the Navy Flight Demonstration Squadron ("Blue Angels"), everyone knows it is their responsibility and duty to speak up if they disagree or if they see an issue that needs to be resolved. This applied in the air as well as on the ground as we move rapidly through our hectic schedules of meetings, briefings, flying, and debriefings. Woe be to someone who recognized a problem and didn't speak up while flying, during a debrief, or a decision meeting.

An emphasis on candor is supported by a culture of respect for differences of opinion and the value in getting all the cards on the table. The leader nurtures a culture of candor by ensuring everyone has the opportunity to be heard. When a contrary view is expressed, it is welcomed and given consideration. We had a ritual at the end of each meeting. We would "go around the room," with each attendee given an opportunity for a final comment before a decision was made or the meeting was adjourned.

Someone sitting silent with an opposing view risks the team making a bad decision and is the organizational version of aerodynamic drag on an airplane. At best, we would be accepting undue risk; at worst, there are significant negative consequences. I read of a leader who when making a decision would assume that silence was disagreement. Before deciding, he would ask each person to say whether they agreed or not. If someone disagreed, they'd be asked if they could support the decision. This avoided someone silently feigning agreement and later undermining the decision.

COMMUNICATION TRAINING

Training Exercise #1: Practice the Rule of 3's

The Rule of 3: "omne trium perfectum," means "Everything that comes in threes is perfect." When preparing remarks to your team, it can be challenging to maintain brevity when called to speak, especially with little notice. Nervousness sets in. To be effective in conveying your thoughts such that the audience receives and remembers them, stick to The Rule of 3's: no more than three ideas briefly delivered.

1. Introduction: Tell them what you're going to tell them.

    a. Tell them you have a few, several, or a couple points (no more than three) related to your topic.

2. Message: Tell them.

a. Cover 1–3 clearly separated ideas ("First, Second, Third," or "One, Two, Three.")

b. No more than a minute or two on each.

c. Resist the temptation to assuage your nervousness or insecurity by repeating yourself or going off-script on a tangent.

3. Conclusion: Tell them what you told them.

a. List your point(s) one more time as a succinct review.

b. Tell them you're done, solicit comments, or ask the audience a question to initiate discussion.

Practice organizing your thoughts this way whenever asked to speak in meetings and conversations for the next week. Soon, it will become natural, and your responses will become more effective.

- How often does your team discuss communication?

- Do you work on being clearer, more concise, more direct?

- How do you ensure the intended messages are received by the right people in a timely manner?

- Were the messages people received the same as the messages that were sent?

- How do you know?

Be a HIGH-TRUST Leader:
Communicate clearly, concisely, consistently, and
directly with candor and predictable regularity.

CHAPTER 9
TO TRUST OR NOT TO TRUST

The best way to find out if you can trust somebody is to trust them.

—Ernest Hemingway

Just as it's important to trust someone if they've earned it, so too it's important to know when not to trust someone. The decision resides in the answers to the questions associated with each of the five pillars of trustworthiness. I want my daughters to ask themselves the five questions about the young men who ask them out on dates. Certainly, the number of scams we hear about every day would be reduced if people asked themselves the five critical questions before handing over their money.

1. **Character**. Is this person honorable and truthful?

2. **Commitment**. Are they committed to doing the right thing and a positive relationship? How will they behave if something goes wrong?

3. **Competence**. Do they know what they're talking about? Can they deliver on their promises?

4. **Connection**. Do they understand me and my situation? Do they care?

5. **Communication**. Do I understand them? Are they telling me the full story?

FIVE TRUST BUSTERS

There are a million ways to damage trust in a relationship, in a brand, in a leader. Based on our 5C's model, here are six guaranteed ways to lower your trustworthiness:

1. **Character**. "Don't do as I do, do as I say." When it becomes inconvenient to walk your talk, take the easy path. Only follow the values you say you stand for when it's easy and comfortable. When you are tired, stressed, angry, discouraged, or distracted, forget your credo and those highfalutin' virtues and do what comes naturally. Afterward, console yourself that at least your intentions are good.

2. **Commitment**. When the going gets tough, procrastinate, lose interest, stop showing up, start taking names and defending yourself against criticism by blaming someone or something else. Keep the gossip flowing. Speak the language of the victim.

3. **Competence**. Reject feedback on your performance and avoid trying to learn a new skill. Only listen to people who tell you what you want to hear. You've worked hard to get where you are; you

earned it. No further need to be curious or struggle to get better, that's for more junior folks.

4. **Connection**. Don't bother to listen when someone is trying to share their concerns, interests, or ideas. Yours are more interesting; you've done one better; and you always have the solution to their problems. So, interrupt, hog the microphone, and tell them what to do. If they don't like it, tell yourself that they're close-minded or ungrateful. Pat yourself on the back for showing that you care.

5. **Communication**. Be vague; use jargon that sounds impressive (to you); pontificate; don't worry about being repetitive; and avoid speaking directly to those you are trying to reach. Don't meet in person when you can call; better yet, send an email or text. Conversations are too time-consuming; hitting "send" on an email/text/tweet is so much more efficient and "the way we communicate around here."

Building and maintaining a reputation of being trustworthy requires constant, deliberate, and often uncomfortable effort. We all are occasionally guilty of trust-busting behavior. Be aware of it and strive to improve. The most successful pilots, yachtsmen, and race car drivers monitor their desired route and constantly make small corrections to stay on course.

REMEMBER HOW YOU GOT HERE

During the final team meeting after winning a national championship, Duke University's basketball coach Mike Krzyzewski spoke to his team about teams and individuals who soar to great heights but then fall and never again achieve the same level of excellence and success. He cautioned them about forgetting what it took for them to win the championship: the hard work, personal sacrifice for the team's success, willingness to learn, pulling together after a tough loss, accepting responsibility for their performance, and appreciating the tireless support they received from so many people in their lives.

Success can contribute to a leader's resistance to change and account for counterproductive behaviors. One is our tendency to exaggerate our contribution to the team's success and minimize our role in setbacks and failures. A complementary view is that while we need to be aware of barriers to change due to previous successes, there are contributors to our past successes that we must not forget.

Unfortunately, success often breeds forgetfulness about what it really took to achieve it, which is why highly accomplished leaders can be poor teachers or mentors. Over time, the spoils of success can sabotage trust in a leader in the following ways:

Character. With success comes more opportunities; they over commit, become distracted with all the attention, and lose connection to the values that contributed to their success.

Commitment. They no longer share in the team's sacrifices. When the team is facing a storm, they can't be counted on to show up, roll up their sleeves, and lead them through the crisis.

Competence. They lose relevance because they stop suffering the pains of continuous learning and adaptation. They become overly protective of their ego and status and are unwilling to keep up with changes in technology, the market, and the environment.

Connection. They lose touch with the people who helped make their success possible. They take them for granted and lose connection by not bothering to stay in touch.

Communication. With all the distractions that success brings, they presume communication has occurred when it hasn't and stop transmitting before the team has received the message. They blame the team for not listening.

WHEN TRUST IS LOST

The Blue Angels selection process seeks to identify trustworthy candidates who will get along well together. However, in the crucible of intense pre-season training followed by months on the road together, the Blue Angels are not immune from personality differences that can affect the team's atmosphere and performance. Speaking to former Blues who served throughout the squadron's 78-year history, it's apparent that all Blue Angels teams face adversity of one kind or another. Occasionally that adversity is born out of interpersonal relationships that become strained due to misunderstandings, differences of opinion, fatigue, and the demands of serving in a dynamic 24/7/365 organization. No different than any high performance team.

The Blue Angels' success in dealing with this natural occurrence when people are working closely together under intense pressure is based on two fundamental characteristics of their culture:

1. The candor and transparency of post-flight debriefs has carried over throughout the organization. When something is bothering someone, they are expected to bring it up forthrightly and respectfully with the other person or to the group as appropriate. Rumors, gossip, and cliques can become a cancer that must be dealt with early in a fair and objective manner.

2. The Blue Angels culture prioritizes its common mission over individual differences that could negatively affect camaraderie,

trust, and performance. Allowed to fester, interpersonal friction can lower the team's performance and may become a safety hazard. Sometimes a little intervention to clear the air and help people see the likely consequences of their attitudes and behavior is all that it takes. Only with mutual understanding and perspective can Trust 3.0 be achieved. It doesn't necessarily require that everyone like one another, but they must respect and understand each other.

Can trust be regained after betrayal? Maybe, maybe not. But do it anyway. Trust is a gift. With the gift of trust comes great responsibility. When that gift is used to manipulate or to take advantage, the feeling of betrayal is deep. Betrayal of trust is at the core of so much anguish, fear, anger, disappointment, and discouragement. It is a wound that requires deliberate corrective action over time to heal.

Talk is cheap. A wound caused by behavior can't be healed with words. Many people feel betrayed when someone they trust, such as a boss, colleague, parent, or friend, abuses their power and influence. When trust is violated, intentionally or unintentionally, an apology written by an attorney, a public relations advisor, or an agent won't cut it. It must be clear, concise, direct, and sincere. It must come from you and be delivered in your own voice: "I did it. I regret it. I won't do it again."

But an apology doesn't earn forgiveness. It is simply the first necessary step to begin the work of earning forgiveness. Earning forgiveness takes time. It requires a pattern of behavior over an extended period that shows others that the apology was real. "Do you walk your talk?" If someone can consistently demonstrate trustworthy behavior, the gift of trust may be given again. Maybe. There are no guarantees, but if you are truly sorry, do it anyway. It's worth it.

TRAINING TO RESTORE TRUST

Training Exercise: Establish Connection through Understanding

When two people don't get along, they often stop talking to each other and talk at each other without really listening.

Let's imagine Bob and Dave are in this situation. They don't get along and it has become personal. It is negatively impacting the team's performance as everyone must work around their dislike for each other. You've decided this can't go on any longer.

After speaking with each one individually to assess their commitment to the team and listen to why each can't get along with the other, you call a meeting with just you three in the room.

Open the meeting with general comments about the importance of everyone on the team working together. Share your observations of their behaviors. Point out the impact and consequences of their poor relationship on the team.

Hand each one a blank sheet of paper and ask them to make a list of the specific behaviors that they don't like about the other.

Ask Bob to start and share his list with Dave, one by one. Dave is not allowed to argue, defend, or deny. However, he can ask a couple of questions for clarification to better understand what Bob means. Dave is encouraged to take notes on each one.

When Bob has completed his list. Dave then recites Bob's list until he can describe each of Bob's complaints to Bob's satisfaction.

Then, Dave covers his list with Bob until Bob can describe each of Dave's complaints to Dave's satisfaction.

You then ask them what immediate changes they will make based on what they heard from each other. As you've decided that the situation is no longer acceptable, if either or both refuse to make the necessary changes in their behaviors, you will have to decide what action you will take.

The goal is for Bob and Dave to achieve mutual understanding and change their attitudes and behaviors accordingly. Trust doesn't necessarily mean we like one another; it means we understand and respect one another.

Be a HIGH-TRUST Leader:

Use the questions associated with the five pillars
of trustworthiness to decide whether to trust.

CHAPTER 10
PERSONAL ACTION PLAN

Action is the foundational key to all success.

—Pablo Picasso

Now that you're familiar with the Five Pillars of Trustworthiness (5Cs), it's time to act and begin training to build greater trustworthiness and greater trust with two key relationships.

In the top row, enter today's date, your name, and the names of two people who are important to you: one in your professional life and one in your personal life. They don't have to be the most important, just two relationships that you'd like to improve or deepen.

Column 1 contains a list of the 5Cs and their associated phrases.

Column 2 contains exercises to help build our trust muscles. For each of the 5Cs of Trustworthiness, write down one specific action you could take this week to improve in each area. Don't make it too hard for your first time. We're making a new habit. Make it easily do-able and then build on your success in the weeks ahead.

Columns 3 and 4 provide space for you to name concrete actions you will take to build trust in these key relationships. Write down one specific action you can take this week in each of the 5Cs to communicate to the two people you listed that you are trustworthy.

Below the table are some examples to get you started:

Date: _____	Write your name here:	The name of a key professional relationship:	The name of a key personal relationship:
5Cs of Trustworthiness	Below list one specific action you can take this week to improve in each area of trustworthiness.	Below list one specific action you can take this week in each area to communicate to this person that you are trustworthy.	Below list one specific action you can take this week in each area to communicate to this person that you are trustworthy.
Character I have integrity; I walk my talk.	I can build my character and improve "walking my talk" by:	I can demonstrate I "walk my talk" to this person by:	I can demonstrate I "walk my talk" to this person by:
Commitment I'm fully engaged in good times and bad.	I can build my commitment and become more engaged by:	I can demonstrate my commitment to this person by:	I can demonstrate my commitment to this person by:
Competence I am skilled and relevant through continuous improvement.	I can become more skilled and relevant by:	I can demonstrate my competence to this person by:	I can demonstrate my competence to this person by:
Connection I listen empathically. They believe I understand them.	I can improve my ability to connect with others by:	I can improve my connection to this person by:	I can improve my connection to this person by:
Communication I am clear, concise, consistent, and direct. I verify my messages are received.	I can improve my communication skills by:	I can communicate more effectively with this person by:	I can communicate more effectively with this person by:

*Figure 4 - Visit **HighTrustLeader.com** for a downloadable PDF.*

Below are examples of specific actions to help you develop your trust training plan. Use them to spur your thinking to create actions most appropriate to you and your relationships. Train to build trust through daily practice.

CHARACTER

Walk your talk by living your personal and company values.

- Make a list of your core values and review the company's values.
- Follow the Golden Rule without compromise.
- Give a truth-teller the authority to be candid when your behavior deviates from your values and company values.
- Talk about company values with your team and discuss why they are important.
- Practice doing the right thing, even when it hurts or is inconvenient.
- Recognize others when they set a great example.
- Ask for feedback: "Am I keeping my promises to the team?"

COMMITMENT

Demonstrate your commitment to the relationship and the team's success.

- Spend time writing and refining your personal and professional purpose and mission.
- Help a colleague with a challenging task or short-fused assignment.

- Keep a positive attitude even when the storm is raging.

- Volunteer for a crummy task outside your area of responsibility that the team needs to get done.

- Be on time without fail.

- Be fully engaged in team meetings—no distractions or multitasking. Be present and attentive on conference calls, too!

COMPETENCE

Be a continuous learner to grow and remain relevant. Seek feedback.

- Sign up for a class to gain knowledge in a new area.

- Convene a debrief with your team after a client meeting or important event to discuss how it went, what could have been done better, and next steps.

- Ask teammates what you could do to raise your skills.

- Set a deadline for learning a new skill or completing a training program.

- Seek regular feedback from all angles.

- Try something new every week.

CONNECTION

Increase your level of understanding and empathy.

- Eat lunch with a different member of your team each week. Ask about their role and how they would like to make a bigger contribution.

- Send a handwritten note on each team member's birthday to express your appreciation for their work and support. Be specific.

- Listen more, talk less, and ask open-ended questions to gain greater understanding of others' points of view.

- Ask a junior teammate for their input during a meeting.

- Ask the boss a few open-ended questions to get greater insight into his or her priorities and concerns. On the personal side, substitute spouse or teenager for boss.

- Practice listening to understand. Initiate a conversation where your goal is to listen, not share information or opinion, but only reply with acknowledgement and questions for better understanding. Practice at least once a day.

COMMUNICATION

Cut through the clutter to successfully transmit the message you intend. Check to make sure the message you intended was the one received.

- Keep emails short and to the point. This includes the number of addressees and cc's.

- Never send an email without proofreading and rewording areas of potential misunderstanding.

- Be considerate of others. Never hit "Reply All" to an email without a good reason.

- Ask for acknowledgement to ensure your message was received.

- Ask your team (and spouse) if your actions communicate a different message than your words.

CHAPTER 11
BUILDING A HIGH-TRUST ORGANIZATION

Trust is what makes a team work,
a company work, a society work,
a civilization work.

—Patrick Lencioni

The Blue Angels have been building and sustaining a HIGH-TRUST culture for nearly 80 years. Every year there is a 50% turnover of officers and pilots, and a 33% turnover of enlisted personnel. It's a never-ending effort. Over time, they developed standards, norms, and traditions that make the work easier. This includes recruiting for trustworthiness and processes to effectively assimilate new members into the squadron.

During my two years as a Blue Angel, none of us said we were the best pilots in the Navy and Marine Corps. There were equally talented naval aviators flying off aircraft carriers, amphibious assault ships, and expeditionary airfields around the world day and night, in good weather and bad. But we did believe, with absolute conviction, that we were the best TEAM of pilots in the world.

Likewise, our entire Blue Angels squadron, with its extraordinary support personnel and maintenance team, achieved things far beyond what any of us previously would have thought possible because we were a team of common people with an uncommon devotion to a core value of HIGH-TRUST.

The five pillars of trustworthiness and their associated questions listed in each chapter also apply to your organization. Just because an organization is made of HIGH-TRUST individuals doesn't ensure that the organization will be viewed as trustworthy. For example, I can think of a large telecommunications company that I don't trust. Each employee I interact with seems trustworthy, but the organization fails in all five pillars:

- **Character.** It doesn't walk its talk. Its actions don't match its marketing, advertising, or company values highlighted on its website. The endless fine print makes me wonder if I can believe its offering.

- **Commitment.** It's not committed to customer service when I'm having problems. It makes me go through Byzantine layers of phone menus and hours of being on hold while trying to deflect my query to its website or chat with a bot that doesn't have a programmed answer to my problem.

- **Competence.** Its service is spotty and expensive. I can't depend on it.

- **Connection.** It feels more interested in efficiency and its profit than serving customers. Its pricing is confusing, constantly changing, and shows no loyalty to established customers.

- **Communication.** Long waits to speak to representatives on the phone or in the stores. Confusing service plans and pricing. It would rather I go to their confusing website than speak to a person. When I finally get to a person, they are in an overseas call center. Their accent and lack of fluency in my language makes it difficult for me to understand them.

WHAT DOES IT TAKE TO BUILD A HIGH-TRUST CULTURE?

Why Do Relatively Few Organizations Do It?

It's simple but not easy. You already know what it takes, but knowledge isn't enough. Action is required!

Vision. A clear target is necessary to inspire, focus your efforts, and set priorities.

Persistence & patience. It will take longer than you imagine but think of it in terms of compound interest. Small regular improvements over time achieve massive results.

Unwillingness to compromise. Adapt and innovate, adjust the means, but not the standards, vision, and commitment to excellence.

The work is never done. But it's the most satisfying work you can do.

The Characteristics of a HIGH-TRUST Culture

Dedicated to a collective purpose or mission. Bigger than what people could accomplish individually. Willing to sacrifice for the team's success.

Everyone is a leader. The work of leadership is too important to leave to top management. Everyone must lead by example with continuous improvement in their area of responsibility and growth in the 5Cs of trustworthiness.

Hold each other accountable. Give and receive the gift of feedback routinely and effectively from all directions to live up to our shared standards and reach our potential. Team accountability is the shared responsibility of all.

Grounded by shared standards. Rules vs. standards. Standards define our identity and values; rules are for protection from the untrustworthy. Rules-based cultures are transactional ("What am I allowed to do?"). Standards-based cultures are transformational ("What should I do?").

10 Actions to Build a HIGH-TRUST Culture

1. YOU must tirelessly set the example in word and deed.

2. Find a cadre of **HIGH-TRUST** people and gradually build outward. Among the right people, excellence is contagious.

3. Establish clear standards as a group with:

   a. Agreed upon objective metrics

   b. Specified desired behaviors

   c. Shared aspirational goals and values

4. Rinse and repeat the message regularly with consistency.

    a. Don't tire of transmitting before the audience absorbs the message.

    b. They won't believe you mean it until you prove otherwise.

5. Recognize your genuine believers. You'll get what you publicize and reward.

    a. Give public shout-outs to people and how they specifically demonstrated the team's shared values.

    b. Be creative. Money is something, but not everything.

    c. Never underestimate the power of authentic public recognition.

6. Lead and coach with stories.

    a. Every company has a story that its employees tell at the water cooler.

    b. What's your company's story?

    c. Tell a compelling and inspirational story about the company's purpose, vision, founding, struggles, and achievements that illustrate its values and standards.

    d. Reinforce values with examples. Publicly describe a teammate who demonstrated a core value or standard in their actions. It communicates and reinforces desired behaviors among the entire team.

7. Empower execution at every level.

    a. High-performance requires speed, adaptability, and energy.

    b.   Ensure transparency and shared awareness.

    c.   Specify, delegate, and grow each person's decision space.

8.   Not everyone will buy in. Cast out the non-believers.

    a.   Give them reasonable time to climb aboard with coaching and constructive feedback.

    b.   "This organization is no longer a good fit for you."

    c.   Move them out (probably sooner than you'd like to). The rest of the team is wondering what is taking you so long.

    d.   A team is not a family. You don't have to put up with a crazy, toxic relative.

9.   Instill rigorous, regular accountability.

    a.   The good ones want it. They like everyone being held accountable and recognized fairly.

    b.   There's a lesson in every mistake and failure. Focus on the lesson.

    c.   Spread the opportunity to improve. Take some medicine yourself.

10. Make trustworthiness a non-negotiable core value.

    a.   For individuals, make trustworthiness the critical basis for hiring, work assignments, promotions, recognition, and compensation.

    b.   For the company, keep asking, "Is our company trusted by its employees, customers, vendors, and partners?" If you truly ask the questions, you may be surprised at the answers.

    c.   Recruit and hire for character and the rest of the five pillars of HIGH-TRUST. Ask how they specifically demonstrated each one in their previous job. Check with their references.

The work is never done, but it's the most satisfying work you can do.

HIGH-TRUST Leaders Are Confident, Not Arrogant

If the Blue Angels walked into the room, you would notice something expected and unexpected. As expected, they are very confident, with a genuine belief in their own skills and abilities. Not because they are natural-born pilots, but rather, through dedicated effort and perfect practice, they know they can perform at a very high level, day-in and day-out. If confronted with an unexpected event in the air, they can prioritize (1. Aviate, 2. Navigate, 3. Communicate) and solve the problem. They aren't afraid to challenge themselves. They know they won't get it right the first 2, 3, 4, or maybe even 10 times. But they prepare before each attempt and seek rigorous, specific feedback to drive improvement. Like a sailboat setting a new course, they make smaller and smaller adjustments as they continually refine their performance.

Here's what many people find unexpected when they meet the Blue Angels: they are humble. Not in an "aw-shucks," weak-kneed way, but in a curious, engaged, interested, selfless manner. They won't hesitate to ask a question, seek advice, or inquire about a better way to do something. They are more concerned with learning and improvement than they are about someone else developing a perception that they don't fit an image of perfection. They are totally unafraid to admit what they don't know. They acknowledge their weaknesses. They don't claim to be perfect and are transparent with their own flaws while trying to improve them. It's their poised confidence combined with genuine self-awareness of areas for improvement that makes them so appealing.

Arrogance, on the other hand, is confidence gone too far. It's an offensive display of superiority and self-importance. This is the boss who thinks he is smarter than everyone else and doesn't think he has anything left to learn or has no need to listen. It's the colleague who cares only about her own rating and views the world as a zero-sum game. It's the consultant who continually interrupts the client to show how much he knows. It's the insecure COO who hoards information in an effort to protect his position, preclude dissent, and appear indispensable.

Be a Smooth Leader

What could my learning to be a successful flight leader have to do with being a successful leader on the ground? Everything.

How many leaders do you know who, when promoted to become the "big cheese," feel they now have the prerogative to change direction and shift gears whenever they desire and it's up to everyone else on the team to keep up? They often hoard information—either due to insecurity or insensitivity—so the team is always in a reactive state of partial understanding. As the boss, they believe everyone else should follow their lead and share their priorities and intentions.

As the leader of the Blue Angels flight team, my main responsibility was to perform high-speed aerobatics in the #1 jet with smoothness and predictability. This allowed my wingmen to fly in incredibly close formation, demonstrating their superior piloting skills to the world.

There were three keys to becoming a smooth flight leader:

1. **Standardization**. We had an established flight routine that I adhered to unless there was a reason to make a change. Standardization drove predictability in routine matters and freed-up our precious attention for high-value opportunities and high-risk situations.

2. **Transparency**. I continually updated the wingmen on where we were and where we were going, so they always had "situational awareness." Armed with this awareness, they could take the initiative to adapt and perform at their best.

3. **Communication**. I was clear, concise, consistent, and direct in giving commands of preparation and execution during each maneuver. My actions exactly matched my words.

Being smooth doesn't mean not being an agile or dynamic leader. As a trusted and effective leader, you can make quick and positive changes, and your team will follow your lead closely. In fact, being smooth in your leadership approach can inspire confidence and trust in your team, allowing them to feel supported and motivated to achieve their best work. This can ultimately lead to a more cohesive and successful team dynamic.

If you're not smooth, your wingmen will hesitate, separate, resist change, and disengage. You may find yourself alone and frustrated, wondering why your team isn't following you with enthusiasm, energy, and full engagement.

Be a smooth leader and allow your team to show the world how great they are.

HIGH-TRUST *Teams Deal with Change and Challenges*

High performance individuals, businesses and organizations are like sharks—they must keep moving forward to survive and succeed--adapting and improving, pushing the limits, and taking advantage of unexpected opportunities.

You can't be successful if you don't take risks, which will naturally involve mistakes, setbacks, and miscues. So, a relevant question is: How do you preserve trust when pushing the limits, adapting to change, and taking risks?

When there is low trust, setbacks and mistakes usually result in defensiveness, finger-pointing, avoiding blame, and political spin to deflect attention from the core causes and issues. Effective learning from mistakes is a resultant casualty.

When there is HIGH-TRUST, mistakes and failures are addressed objectively. Individuals, and just as importantly, the team accepts responsibility. Creative solutions are found. Enthusiasm is preserved while confidence and initiative are restored. Through a process of continual learning, competency increases, so does confidence—individually and collectively— and trust grows as a result.

It's Not the Plan, It's the Planning

Far too often I see leaders who are "winging it," making decisions on the fly, in the heat of the moment, without a plan or a map. Oh, they did some planning in the beginning, but that was a while ago, before they got busy.

HIGH-TRUST Leaders believe in regularly putting the brakes on to slow down, get in the slow lane, and take the time to ask the hard questions: "What is our purpose? Our vision? Our strategies?" "What relevant objectives will we measure?" Only after asking these questions do they ask, "What is the work that needs to be done?"

Mediocre leaders say they don't have time for that stuff. "We don't follow the plan anyway, so why bother?" These weak leaders lack courage: the courage and discipline to develop an effective plan that requires unvarnished self-awareness of their current situation, deep reflection on their ultimate goal or vision, and the high-priority strategies to realize their vision. Amid a crisis, they knee-jerk in order to "make something happen" to stop the pain. They waste valuable assets and squander their team's time and energy as they flail about. Unfortunately, as our parents admonished, haste makes waste. And longer-term success is often sacrificed to ameliorate short-term painful symptoms. Granted, plans usually must be adjusted and modified, sometimes significantly. A great leader understands the need for flexibility during execution. And a team that plans well, can modify the plan rapidly.

Here's the payoff that is too often missed: the value of a plan is in the planning, not the product. It's the lessons and insights gained by asking the hard questions and getting clarity on the mission, the vision, the strategies, the objectives, and the details, always the details.

Do you and your team have the courage and discipline to do regular planning? And practice the plan? Including the contingencies? Do you drill down into the "What ifs?" and seek greater detail? Poor planners never get to the details, never do the hard work to anticipate "What if?" contingencies. They assume and hope the plan will go as expected and aren't prepared to adjust effectively, because they didn't arm themselves with "What ifs." Doing the heavy lifting of addressing "What if" contingencies arm the leader and their team with the ability to seize the initiative when an opportunity presents itself and react quickly when faced with adversity. It positively impacts both the offense and defense and the speed of both—this isn't haste, this is lightning reflexes! This is an All-Pro quarterback calling an audible at the line of scrimmage and throwing a touchdown pass into a gap in coverage; this is the champion basketball team not taking a time-out with seconds remaining, instead pushing the ball up the floor to win at the buzzer as their frozen opponents fail to react until it's too late.

Do you and your team have the courage and discipline to do regular planning? Do you practice and review the plan? Do you include the contingencies?

Do you drill down into the "What ifs" and seek greater detail? How will you recognize an unforeseen opportunity? An unexpected set-back? Have you coordinated your responses with your partners?

Is everyone on the team familiar with the plan? Or is the plan too valuable to someone's position and influence to share with their teammates?

What have you learned from your planning that you can use to update and improve your current processes and policies?

Have you shared your lessons with the rest of your organization? Or are they too busy to slow down and listen? If so, why?

TRUST AND DELEGATION

Many corporate executives believe they must single-handedly generate solutions and offer responses. They want to be kept informed about every little thing and don't clearly define the responsibilities and limits of their people's authority (decision space). This results in the leader having to give permission for nearly every decision, underutilizing the team around them, lacking the trust necessary to allow team members to rise to the occasion. The team is then unable to brainstorm collectively, be heard, speak candidly, face realities head-on, and take the initiative to solve problems early or seize valuable opportunities quickly.

An Air Force F-15 fighter pilot once told me the story of a preflight briefing between a cocky, seasoned flight leader and a brand-new wingman.

Flight Leader-A began by asking, "Why are you here?"

The rookie wingman nervously responded, "Well, I've always loved aircraft and the idea of serving my country—"

"No, no, no," the leader interrupted, "You're here because my jet only has one radar and can only carry eight missiles!"

The message was: "I have to put up with you because I can't do it all by myself."

In contrast, Flight Leader-B views his wingman as a tactical partner who brings added expertise, creativity, and another perspective to the mission. He delegates responsibility and authority to his wingman to achieve a higher level of performance, adaptability, and survivability.

Which wingman feels more trusted? Which wingman will give more commitment, loyalty, and engagement?

Flight Leader-A doesn't value his wingman and views delegation as a price he's not willing to pay.

Flight Leader-B views respect and delegation as an investment that offers compound interest.

Effective delegation is not efficient. It requires time, attention, energy, patience, and a willingness to accept that the project, mission, or task may likely be accomplished differently than the leader would have done it. Delegation = Trust. Earlier, I described how I delegated the responsibility to visually inspect my jet before every flight to my crew chief. Could you fully trust a direct report with something critical and not check their work?

To delegate effectively, the leader must:

- Clearly communicate expectations, priorities, and the desired outcome (the Navy calls it "Commander's Intent").
- Specify responsibilities and authority (decision space) and restrictions or limitations ("rules of engagement").
- Provide proper training and adequate resources.
- Be available for questions and provide clarification.
- Be generous with encouragement and authentic praise.
- Accept that mistakes will happen. It's worth it if learning is involved.

Some leaders are not willing to let go and trust their teammates. Micromanagers often justify their behavior by using excuses like, "I have high standards," or "I don't have time to teach." Micromanagers prefer the illusion of control, but a micromanaged team will never achieve its full potential.

Leaders should prioritize the work that only they can do. Anything else should be delegated to others. **HIGH-TRUST** Leaders recognize the time invested in training their teammates today will result in massive time savings with much greater results in the future. Effective delegation is a force multiplier!

Be a HIGH-TRUST Leader: Take the time and do the hard work to delegate successfully and watch your team soar to new heights.

TRUST AND DIVERSITY

The crew on a Navy aircraft carrier consists of nearly 5,000 men and women, from all walks of life in America: all races, ethnicities, religions, economic backgrounds, and experiences. They come together under a common mission and shared sacrifice to operate in unison in one of the world's most dynamic and dangerous environments: the flight deck of an aircraft carrier. They work day and night in all seasons and weather, often thousands of miles from land for eight months or more. It is the shared mission and sacrifice, directed by principled leaders, that strengthens not only the crew's bond but also their ability to navigate complex challenges with agility and resilience. Their collective efforts enable the aircraft carrier to project power and protect national interests across the globe.

Diversity can play a huge role in achieving organizational success. If we all act the same, look the same, read the same books, view the same media, see the world the same, share a common history and life experiences, our team will be limited in what it can accomplish. Diversity brings a variety of viewpoints and perspectives with fresh ideas and new connections between old ideas. It helps prevent blind spots and unexpected surprises.

But we also know that diversity brings its own challenges. There is no free lunch. It brings an inherent tendency toward misunderstandings which result in lower levels of trust. To unlock the great benefits of diversity, leaders must make a sizable investment with their two most valuable resources: their time and attention. They must slow down and take time to connect, to ensure that everyone feels understood.

When we're all the same, we can go fast because we speak the same language and we essentially see the world the same way. You already know what everyone is thinking because they think like you. Speed is valuable, but it brings risk and comes at a cost. Build the team with people just like you and pay the price with limited upside and risky blind spots that can cause unexpected surprises, such as rapidly going over a cliff. Build the team with people of various backgrounds, experiences, and geolocations, and make a significant investment in building and maintaining CONNECTION to reap the rewards of diversity.

Recognize that diversity requires more effort. It's worth it.

Training to Leverage Diversity

Invite the person on your team who is most different from you to lunch and devote the occasion to simply listening to their thoughts, ideas, and suggestions. Be in the receive-only mode. See what you learn and how your relationship deepens.

CHAPTER 12
ADDITIONAL THOUGHTS

You must never confuse faith that you will prevail in the end—which you can never afford to lose—with the discipline to confront the most brutal facts of your current reality, whatever they might be.

—Vice Admiral James Stockdale[10]

IT STARTS WITH YOU

So, you want to be a HIGH-TRUST Leader? And you want to develop a HIGH-TRUST culture to truly achieve exceptional results with a high-performance organization? Well, then, you must go first. Your team will never achieve HIGH-TRUST if you don't lead

---

[10] Vice Admiral James Stockdale, USN (1923–2005) was awarded the Medal of Honor for heroic action as the senior prisoner of war during the Vietnam War.

the way and embody the change, the values, and the behavior you desire. It's as simple—and hard—as that.

>**Character**. Eliminate the hypocrisy between your words, values, intentions, and actions.

>**Commitment**. Be clear about your purpose and respond every day with resolve to show you are dedicated to achieving long-term goals and will not be derailed by short-term temptations and crises.

>**Competence**. Demonstrate a learner's mindset to develop new skills that enhance your performance. This will require delegating some of the comfortable stuff you like doing to free up time and energy to learn new, relevant skills.

>**Connection**. If you want them to understand you, you must take the time to understand them. They won't truly listen to what you think until they believe you understand and care about them.

>**Communication**. Leading by example is the most powerful form of communication. Turn down the emphasis on words and let your actions shout loud and clear.

If you want them to change, you have to change first. Show them the way with your personal example. It is the only way that lasts. Anything else is a mirage.

Be a HIGH-TRUST Leader: Go first. Lead from the front. Set the example. Be the change you want to see in the organization. They will give you credit and forgive missteps if they see you are genuinely trying to change and don't give up.

THE STOCKDALE PARADOX: REALISTIC OPTIMISM

HIGH-TRUST Leaders are respected and admired for their ability to stay true to their values and purpose amid the ups and downs of business cycles and the storms of life we all face.

> **Character**. They walk their talk, living their values, even when tempted to sacrifice their integrity to relieve some of the pain in a storm.
>
> **Commitment**. They remain focused on their mission and long-term purpose. Even when battling alligators, they remember their goal is to drain the swamp.
>
> **Competence**. They adapt and grow, seeing challenges and storms as learning opportunities to improve their performance.
>
> **Connection**. They stay in touch with their teammates, showing understanding and empathy for their problems and welcoming their ideas and suggestions.
>
> **Communication**. They're transparent about their own concerns and uncertainty while inspiring their team that they will succeed.

But there is another character skill they possess: realistic optimism. The ability and the discipline to see the truth in every situation; the whole truth—the bad and the good.

Vice Admiral James Stockdale was a HIGH-TRUST leader par excellence. As the senior prisoner of war (POW) in Vietnam, he shouldered a nearly unimaginable burden of command. In his famous book on outstanding businesses, *Good to Great*, Jim Collins discussed "The Stockdale Paradox":

Tortured over 20 times during his eight-year imprisonment from 1965 to 1973, Stockdale lived out the war without any prisoner's rights, no set release date, and no certainty as to whether he would even survive to see his family again. He shouldered the burden of command, doing everything he could to create conditions that would increase the number of prisoners who would survive unbroken, while fighting an internal war against his captors and their attempts to use the prisoners for propaganda.

Stockdale described his leadership secret: "I never lost faith in the end of the story . . . I never doubted not only that I would get out, but also that I would prevail in the end and turn the experience into the defining event of my life, which, in retrospect, I would not trade . . . This is a very important lesson. You must never confuse faith that you will prevail in the end, which you can never afford to lose, with the discipline to confront the most brutal facts of your current reality, whatever they might be."

The Stockdale Paradox carries an important lesson in character development, a lesson in faith and honesty: never doubt you can achieve your goals, no matter how lofty they may be and no matter what naysayers and critics may say. But at the same time, always take honest stock of your current situation. Don't lie to yourself for fear of short-term embarrassment or discomfort because such deception will come back to defeat you in the end.

Living the first half of this paradox is relatively easy since optimism really isn't that hard. You just choose to believe it will all turn out for the best and everything that happens to you is a means to that end. But optimism on its own can be dangerous. An optimist who says, "No need to act, everything will OK," can be just as big a problem as a pessimist who says, "It's all futile, why bother?" Both perspectives result in inaction.

We need to embrace the second half of the Stockdale Paradox to really make strides. Of course, nobody likes admitting they need to exercise more, they're broke, they've chosen the wrong career, or their marriage is falling apart. But admitting such truths is an absolute necessity if you want to grow and improve. It might feel like you are taking a few steps backward by doing so, but view that retreat as the pull-back on a slingshot: you are setting yourself up to make significant progress.

Years ago, I attended a panel discussion of Vietnam POWs at NAS Pensacola that included VADM Stockdale. The moderator asked the former POWs what Stockdale's leadership meant to them. One very tough former POW sitting next to Stockdale began to speak, and then overcome with emotion, he could only reach over and give the admiral a long, firm squeeze on the shoulder. That said it all.

ARE YOU A STRONG FINISHER?

Many self-improvement books and blogs exhort their readers to "Get started," "Ignite," "Initiate action," and "Go for it!" And while taking the first step can be challenging for many, finishing strong is equally (if not more) daunting, especially for talented people with lots of great ideas.

Starting something new is exciting, full of possibilities, with rosy outcomes imagined. Being on the ground floor of a new initiative is intoxicating as excited teammates brainstorm and launch something new. Then, along the way, reality sets in with challenges to overcome, unexpected delays and frustrations, the inherent friction and elbow grease required to turn great ideas into something tangible that delivers value. Over time, the sheen wears off amid pressures, criticisms, and fatigue as you face what author Steven Pressfield refers to as "Resistance."

Meanwhile, we are deluged with new ideas, new info, new opportunities. And because we're talented and love considering possibilities, we take our eye off the current, ongoing project or task and our energy required for completion becomes dissipated. We may get to the finish line, but it's not the crescendo of success we had imagined at the beginning. Lots of "productive people" are energetic starters, but poor finishers. Often, they're simply too busy.

FIGHT THE GOOD FIGHT

HIGH-TRUST Leaders are in a fight every day to live according to the five pillars. It is a good fight, a noble fight, but a fight nonetheless. They accept it as the natural order of things. They don't look the other way, make excuses, or wish it was otherwise. It is a fight they welcome as the path to breaking out of the pack, to be memorable, to make a difference. It is a fight waged within themselves because they are human.

If you are a HIGH-TRUST Leader who is given an important mission, everyone wants to go with you, to be part of something important with someone they trust. If you can't find good people, well, look in the mirror. Who are you reflecting? Who are you attracting? In order to be trusted, you must be trustworthy.

Are you here to win or are you here to play? When pressure, time constraints, deadlines, and the environment conspire to entice the HIGH-TRUST Leader to compromise on values, to take the short-cut, to tell herself, "Just this once," they fight the relentless temptation to take a slice out of their character and integrity by fighting back.

Be a HIGH-TRUST Leader:

Go first, remember the Stockdale Paradox, and finish strong.

CHAPTER 13
AFTERWORD

I n November 1998, I was on the dais in the Blue Angels Atrium at the National Naval Aviation Museum for our change of command ceremony. Admiral Jay Johnson, the Chief of Naval Operations (CNO) was sitting on one side and CDR Patrick Driscoll, who would soon be taking my place, on the other. I looked out across the large audience that included my extended family and friends from Western Pennsylvania, college friends, and shipmates from previous squadrons and deployments. Standing in formation were the squadron's officers and chief petty officers, and manning the rail above me were the Blue Angels Sailors and Marines. Everyone was in service dress uniforms and looked like they materialized out of a recruiting poster. Frankly, I missed much of CNO's remarks as I couldn't help looking at each of my teammates and thinking about all we had been through together. Tomorrow's airshow would be our last and then our time together would be over—a season is a lifetime. The next day, the 1999 Team would be born and begin its journey.

Words can't describe how much I admire and appreciate all my teammates. In the air, we flew as well as any Blue Angels team, pushing our limits every weekend, including adding two new maneuvers—the F/A-18 Diamond Landing and the Half-Cuban Eight on Takeoff—and we did it safely with zero mishaps. Our C-130 Fat Albert pilots and crews met every logistic requirement and thrilled airshow spectators with their flight demonstration and Jet-Assisted Takeoff (JATO).

The support officers and enlisted personnel were the finest I could imagine. Most went on to distinguished Navy and Marine careers, making a positive impact everywhere they went. Others transitioned to successful civilian careers and became leaders in their communities.

Each and every day, ordinary people do extraordinary things. That pretty much sums up our '97–'98 Blue Angels Teams. We were ordinary people dedicated to an uncompromising value of trustworthiness that led to extraordinary accomplishments. It was the hardest work we've ever done—and it was magic.

I'm glad to be here.

Captain George Dom, USN(Ret)

Appendix I
Trust Rules

Building and sustaining a high level of trust is the sine qua non of leadership and teamwork. Without it, there is frustration, discouragement, and disengagement. With it, even the sky isn't the limit. When it comes to relationships, trust rules.

1. Trust is the glue for all relationships.

2. Trust is a reward that must be earned every day.

3. In order to be trusted, you must be trustworthy.

4. When evaluating your own trustworthiness, your opinion is interesting, but not sufficient. Truth-tellers are vital for feedback.

5. Five interdependent pillars of trustworthiness (5C's) are:

    Character. "Do you walk your talk?"

    Commitment. "Will you be there when times are tough and play to win?"

    Competence. "Are you skilled enough and relevant?"

    Connection. "Do they believe you understand them?"

    Communication. "Are you clear, concise, and direct? Was your message received?"

6. In all high-performance teams, a HIGH-TRUST culture is a strategic imperative, both individually and collectively. HIGH-

TRUST Teams recruit for trustworthiness; they train to build it every day and hold each other accountable; they promote based on it; they recognize and reward trustworthiness; and they will fire or sideline someone quickly if trust is irreparably lost.

7.   When trust grows, so does engagement, speed, productivity, quality, creativity, innovation, morale, retention, and resilience. When trust goes up, costs go down.

8.   Leaders are responsible for building a **HIGH-TRUST** culture. Everyone must be a leader in building their own trustworthiness and the team's culture of trust.

9.   The team is looking for the leader to go first, to set the example. They are watching closely. You can't lead anyone farther than you've led yourself.

10.   There is a power of attraction to **HIGH-TRUST** Leaders and Teams.

 ‣   If you are considered very trustworthy, everyone wants you on their team. They want you to help seize the opportunity or resolve the crisis.

 ‣   And when you are given an important mission as a **HIGH-TRUST** Leader, everyone wants to be on your team. They want to do great things being led by someone they trust.

11.   No matter how good a relationship or a team is, it can always get better by deepening the level of trust. Getting to the next level of success requires getting to the next level of trust and confidence. This work is never over.

Appendix II
Briefing and Flying a Blue Angels Airshow

Figure 5 - 1997 Blue Angels Jet Demo Pilots: L-R: LT Scott "Yogi" Beare (#6), LCDR Ryan "Doc" Scholl (#5), LCDR Scott "Scooter" Moyer (#4), LT Mark "Gucci" Dunleavy (#3), MAJ Pat "Kato" Cooke (#2), CDR George "Boss" Dom (#1).

Figure 6 – View of the Blue Angels Delta formation from below.

The Preflight Briefing

Arrival and Briefing Room. Upon arrival at the airport, the officers met in a conference room. Only the current team, former Blue Angels, honorary Blue Angels, and special guests could enter the briefing room. It was a sanctuary to remove distractions, so the Team could fully focus on the upcoming flight. As each person entered the room, they greeted each of their teammates with a handshake—a greeting ritual that reinforced connection and camaraderie.

The Preflight Briefing. Five minutes prior to the scheduled start time, conversations became hushed as everyone settled into their usual seats at the conference table and along the perimeter of the room.

Delta Briefing. All pilots and support officers were present. At precisely the scheduled time, I welcomed any former and honorary Blue Angels and then briefed the overall flight plan, including weather and winds forecast; bearing and range to the nearest divert field; safe ejection area; radio channels, duty runway, taxi formation, and route to the runway. Referencing my photo of the airport, I would step through all the maneuvers using my pen to depict the flight profiles in relation to CenterPoint.

Visualization. During the 6-plane Delta maneuvers, the demo pilots would "chair-fly" some of the maneuvers. As I recited the radio calls, we would each visualize flying the maneuver with closed eyes, simulating moving the control stick and throttles, looking left or right, thinking of correcting any errors made on the previous flight. I would review my checkpoints, power settings, radio calls, and think about how the winds would affect the maneuvers.

Kato (#2; NATOPS[11] Officer) would announce an immediate action emergency procedure. All pilots would recite the action steps in unison from memory.

Scooter (#4; Training Officer) would highlight a few maneuvers from the last few flights that needed work for continued improvement.

Doc (#5; Ops Officer) would add a comment or two for emphasis.

Each pilot would announce a specific goal for the flight— one maneuver identified during the previous debrief that needed improvement.

I would end this portion of the briefing with "Diamond, Solos, Bert, Narrator, Comm Cart, and Tower, let's have a good one!"

The support officers then headed to their respective stations—comm cart, control tower, announcer's stand— the Solos (#5, #6) and the Bert pilots found quiet rooms to brief the detailed specifics of their maneuvers while the Diamond pilots (#1–#4) remained in the conference room for their detailed briefing of the Diamond portion of the flight demonstration.

At the appointed time, the demo pilots would be driven in a van to the jets parked in front of the crowd to avoid a long walk and distractions. We would be dropped off next to the

---

[11] Naval Air Training and Operating Procedures Standardization (NATOPS)

#6 jet to watch Bert's flight demonstration. After Bert's high-speed, low altitude pass, we walked behind the jets, in order, greeting and shaking the hands of the Crew Chiefs and Mechs until we reached the #1 jet to watch our USMC teammates complete their C-130 demo. I'll be honest, the large crowds, coupled with our responsibility to represent the Navy and Marine Corps, and to uphold the Blue Angel legacy gave me butterflies before every performance. But after greeting each one of the enlisted Crew Chiefs and Mechs, shaking their hands, looking in their eyes, and hearing each one say, "Have a good one, Boss!", I was fired-up, confident, and ready to go!

FLYING #1 (LEAD JET): CDR GEORGE "BOSS" DOM, USN

Figure 7 - Delta formation with #1 highlighted.

Description and Responsibilities

In addition to my responsibilities as the commanding officer of the squadron, I was the leader of the flight demonstration. From the moment I climbed into my jet until our salute to the crowd to end the demonstration, the timing and placement of every maneuver depended on the profile I flew in the air and taxied on the ground.

Stick and Rudder: Flying the #1 (Leader's) Position

The wingmen depended on me to be as consistent as possible despite the terrain, obstructions, wind, and weather conditions, so they could fly as close as humanly possible to my jet, rendezvous expeditiously for the next maneuver, and become totally in sync with me and each other. This required intense repetition in training to make every power setting, every turn, every roll and pull as consistent as possible. Detailed study was required to rapidly become familiar with a different show site every weekend. There were no computers that flew the jets or GPS to navigate—each of us flew by precise eye-hand coordination and steely concentration. We navigated by visual reference to checkpoints on the ground.

Talking and Flying. To taxi and fly in unison only a couple feet apart required all the pilots to move the controls in their cockpits simultaneously—throttles, control stick, speedbrake, rudder pedals, and smoke activation. The minimum separation between the jets does not allow the wingmen time to see the leader's jet move and then respond. I would make radio calls before moving the throttles or any flight control so the wingmen could match me in unison.

Rolling. To roll the formation 360 degrees, I'd transmit a drawn-out OK: "OoooooooK." "Ooooooo" allowed them to prepare for the roll, and exactly on the "K" we would all move our control sticks to the left, and the jets would roll together as the wingmen continually made small corrections to stay in position. I would smoothly increase the rate of roll for the first 90 degrees. Whatever rate of roll I had achieved at 90 degrees had to be maintained for the remaining 270 degrees. The roll rate would determine how much altitude we gained and lost during the maneuver, so I would adjust as needed to remain under any clouds or to avoid any obstructions on our flight path on the ground.

Looping. Flying a loop in formation required entering the maneuver with enough speed to safely get over the top and maintain maneuverability. Pulling back on the control stick to initiate the climb required a smooth and consistent application of G-force so the wingmen could match me and each other. My radio calls for a looping maneuver were, "Up we go. A little more pull. Adding power." On the "g" in go, we'd all pull back on our control sticks in unison. "A little more pull" helped them continue to match me. On the "p" in "Adding power" we'd all move our throttles forward to sustain energy on the jets. My jet had a metal plate on the throttle quadrant that prevented me from moving the throttle all the way forward. This gave the wingmen a power advantage needed to catch up if they fell slightly behind.

Most Difficult Maneuver: Diamond Landing

All the maneuvers required mind-numbing concentration and precision, including formation changes behind the crowd while navigating to set up for the next maneuver. The Left Echelon Roll and the Line Abreast Loop both demanded I fly a rock-solid profile as they were very difficult maneuvers for the wingmen to shift into position as well as fly the maneuvers. In my second year, we landed four jets together in the Diamond formation. I couldn't relax my concentration on the final maneuver of the demonstration as we flew a tight visual pattern in formation while we extended the landing gear and flaps in unison, established a 3-degree glideslope, and hit the touchdown point precisely on centerline. Gucci (#4) in the slot behind me would be the first to land, then Weeds (#2) and Wolfy (#3).[12] I was the last to land with my tailpipes coming down in front of Gucci (#4) while he was adding power to maintain the Diamond formation. Once we were all on deck, I called for braking in unison to come to a stop together in formation. A wonderful demonstration of teamwork: four pilots flying as one from takeoff to landing: E Quattuor Unum: Four as One!

Memorable Airshow Story: Buzzing the USAF Thunderbirds

During my second year, we flew a July 4 airshow over Traverse City, MI. The Thunderbirds were performing nearby that weekend in Battle Creek, MI. Sunday morning, Yogi (#5) called the FAA and extended the Tbirds' FAA airshow waiver for 30 minutes. After we finished our demo in Traverse City, we launched and headed for Battle Creek. The Thunderbird pilots were signing autographs at the crowd line after their show when the audience looked north and saw us coming head-on at low altitude in our 6-plane Delta formation with the smoke on! We overflew the crowd, turned around to show them a Delta Roll, followed by our signature Fleur de Lis looping maneuver. We ended with a very low pass down the runway in tight formation with our smoke billowing over the Thunderbirds' F-16 jets. We then climbed in formation and turned south to return home to Pensacola!

---

[12] For the 1998 season, Maj. Scott "Weeds" Wedemeyer, USMC, replaced Kato as #2 and LT David "Wolfy" Silkey, USN, replaced Gucci as #3, and Gucci moved to the slot position #4.

FLYING #2 (RIGHT WING): MAJ PAT "KATO" COOKE, USMC

Figure 8 - Diamond in right echelon with #2 highlighted

Description and Responsibilities

1. **Set the formation.** The right wing is the team's blue-collar position, requiring dependability and steady hard work. The right wingman is the only pilot on the team who must fly rolling maneuvers on both the right and left side of the formation.

My primary responsibility was to "set" the formation for each maneuver, a specific position relative to the leader's aircraft for the other wingmen to match, to achieve formation symmetry. #2's position changes from maneuver to maneuver and is modified based on the flight conditions. The right wingman must be consistently and reliably in position to provide stability for the other wingmen.

2. **Train the new leader**. The critical role of right wingmen in their second year is to provide the new flight leader with candid, constructive, actionable feedback after every flight, especially during pre-season

training. The two-year tours of duty for the Boss and the right wingman are staggered: when a new Boss joins the team, he will start his training with an experienced second-year #2. Although new flight leaders join the Team with more naval aviation experience than the wingmen, the second-year right wingman has more Blue Angel experience. They train or guide the new flight leader in the early stages of training. This training relationship is unique and doesn't follow a typical "rookie versus veteran" model. The new leader doesn't need to learn how to fly; he needs to learn how to fly with five other jets tucked extremely close under his wings. #2's job is to give the new flight leader the wingman's perspective and feedback on every move he makes in the jet - in the air and on the ground.

Stick and Rudder: Flying the #2 (Right Wing) Position

The wingmen use visual references on the lead aircraft to define their proper position. For the right and left wingmen, these checkpoints are mainly found on the lead aircraft's spine, aft and below its cockpit. While underneath the lead's wing, the wingmen will fly their position by placing the leading edge of the leader's wing on their checkpoint. The checkpoints may be certain letters of the aircraft manufacturer's name stenciled on each aircraft, the head of a bolt, or some other minor feature. Blue Angels call this "flying your paint." Once in position, the wingmen can look at their reference point and quickly determine if they start to drift high (flat), low (deep), forward, aft, or toward or away from the lead (up or down the bearing line). To understand the precision required to be in position, the wingmen may only allow their sight picture to drift a couple of inches before being considered out of position. When a new wingman joins the team, the pilot's visual scan may not be quick enough or precise enough to recognize being out of position. Flying formation using visual checkpoints is easy to understand while flying straight and level in smooth air. Now consider the stick, rudder, and power adjustments required when the formation starts rolling, looping, and encountering bumpy conditions.

Most Difficult Maneuver: Flying in Echelon

When asked what the most difficult maneuver is, most wingmen will say, "They're all difficult!" Indeed, the concentration required throughout a demonstration flight does not change from takeoff to landing. However, some maneuvers employ different formations, which require additional safety precautions. During some maneuvers, the four Diamond pilots shift into the echelon formation with the three wingmen flying in a diagonal line on the same side of the #1 aircraft (see photo above). This echelon formation sandwiches the #2 and #3 aircraft between #1 and #4, leaving little room for error, especially when the formation does an echelon rolling maneuver in bumpy air.

Memorable Airshow Story: Strive For Perfection and Achieve Excellence

Numerous memorable moments occur during a Blue Angel tour of duty, from flying in a six-plane formation in the clouds during an instrument approach to a small-town airport to fireworks exploding near the formation on a flyover of Disney World's Magic Kingdom or flying with your teammates between skyscrapers in Chicago, San Francisco, and Cleveland. There are also great memories of the thousands of hours spent working with and sharing great times with the other officers and enlisted team members. Ultimately, the immense privilege of representing the Navy and Marine Corps with these professionals is what I'll never forget.

However, during my two-year tour on the Team, which included hundreds of practice flights and show demonstrations, two flights stood out as truly exemplary. During two separate shows, one in Seattle and one in San Francisco, everything came together, and we flew as close to a "perfect show" as we ever had. Every person on the Team had their best start-to-finish performance. For those forty-five minutes, all the hard work, struggle to perfect individual performance, and brutally honest debriefs finally paid off. Sometimes, it seemed we would never achieve that level of performance, but it remained our goal. It was a testament to the Blue Angels who preceded us, our trust and belief in one another, and the fighting spirit of those we represent in naval aviation. Those two days were worth it all.

FLYING #3 (LEFT WING): LT MARK "GUCCI" DUNLEAVY, USN

Figure 9 - The Diamond over San Francisco Bay with #3 highlighted

Description and Responsibilities

The Left Wingman (#3) is always a first-year pilot. My primary responsibility was to balance the formation. Kato (#2) on the right wing set the formation, and I was expected to match his position during all the maneuvers. So, while I am flying a couple feet from the #1 (Boss's) aircraft, I must also glance across to match Kato's position.

For my second year, I moved to the slot position as #4, and later recalled to the team to fly as #2 in a third year as a Blue Angel. All positions are very difficult to master, but after flying as #2, #3, and #4, in my humble opinion—with exception of the Boss (#1)—#3 is the most difficult position in the formation. In addition to being a new pilot, all the formation rolling maneuvers are to the left into #3, requiring me to push the control stick forward and left while rolling 360 degrees—something we never did in pilot training or in our fleet squadrons.

Stick and Rudder: Formation Rolls in the #3 (Left Wing) Position

The stick and rudder movements during formation rolling maneuvers on the left wing are counterintuitive. At the beginning of the roll, I had to move the stick to the left precisely on the Boss's call while also reducing power as the formation rolls into me. The Boss would build the roll rate for the first 90 degrees of roll and then maintain that rate for the remaining 270 degrees. I would continue holding forward/left stick to match the Boss while adding power on the backside of the roll and keeping the rudders neutral.

Most Difficult Maneuver: Left Echelon Roll

Kato (#2) highlighted the challenges of flying in echelon. By far, the most difficult maneuver as a first-year pilot in the #3 jet was the Left Echelon Roll. On the Boss's call, "Go left echelon," I had to slide back to make room for Kato (#2) to cross under to the Boss's left wing, leaving me sandwiched between Kato and Scooter (#4). I still had to use the Boss's jet as my reference by flying slightly forward on Kato so I could keep sight of a sliver of the Boss's jet.

Memorable Airshow Story: Double Farvel at Reading, PA

Since the impromptu airshow for the Thunderbirds and the folks at Battle Creek has already been mentioned, I want to share a memory of the airshow weekend at Reading, Pennsylvania. There was a ridgeline southeast of the show site that we had to fly over in a steep descent to commence the maneuvers at the proper altitude in front of the crowd. The Double Farvel is a 4-plane Diamond formation with #1 and #4 upside down. At Reading, the Boss called, "Rolling in," as we were cresting the ridge, he and I rolled our jets upside down in unison. The Diamond descended into the valley with the Boss and I flying upside down with the smoke on, we then pushed negative G to level-off upside down 100 feet above the ground as we passed by the crowd!

San Francisco's Fleet Week and Seattle's Seafair were my two favorite show sites. Two beautiful cities. We were blessed with clear skies both years we flew there. Wonderful memories.

FLYING #4 (SLOT): LCDR SCOTT "SCOOTER" MOYER, USN

Figure 10 - The Double Farvel formation with #4 highlighted

Description and Responsibilities

1. **Safety Officer for the formation.** With #2 and #3 intently focused on the Boss's aircraft to maintain position within incredibly tight parameters, they don't have the ability to check their altitude and airspeed. While the Boss is ultimately responsible for keeping the formation within the altitude and airspeed limits for each maneuver, I backed him up in the event he became distracted and was not within parameters to safely complete a maneuver. I also monitored the wingmen's positions to ensure adequate separation. While they became very skilled at maintaining their positions to fly extremely close to each other (and to the Boss), there was little room for error. I take great pride that in my three years of flying as a Blue Angel, our planes never touched.

During airshows late in the season we had progressed to our tightest formations. As we set-up for the next maneuver, I called for the wingmen to "Take it in" which meant bring their jets in close to the Boss (without touching!). #2 Kato and #3 Gucci would fly their jets into their tightest position from Boss's jet. Literally inches away! I'm in the 'slot' position, watching them come in close and ready to say "spread it" if they become dangerously close.

I would often bite my tongue as I watched their wingtips stop within inches of each other as we were rolling or looping. They were that good! And Boss's profile was that solid!

At the end of every maneuver, after Boss called "smoke off," I would tell the wingmen "Let's ease it out," which meant to take a little separation from Boss so he could aggressively drive the formation to set up for the next maneuver. After a great maneuver, I would use a voice inflection in my call "Lets eeease it out!" to let Boss and the wingmen know that we just nailed it! Nothing in the world like it!

2. **Training Officer.** During Winter Training, I developed daily and weekly training plans to introduce and refine all the airshow maneuvers. I worked closely with Kato (#2) to teach the Boss to consistently fly the maneuvers while training Gucci (#3) and the two solo pilots, Doc (#5) and Yogi (#6), to fly their positions in the 6-plane Delta formation.

I also facilitated the debrief after every flight. It was crucial to ensure there was as much detailed, constructive feedback as possible without letting it get personal or emotional. That can be easier said than done when you have a group of very determined and talented personalities, each striving for perfection!

I thoroughly enjoyed my teaching responsibilities. I loved the challenge of trying to determine what teaching techniques work best for each pilot. Fighter pilots have all sorts of personalities and each respond to coaching differently. We all wanted to do our very best, eager to learn and improve, so finding the most effective way to teach and constructively debrief was challenging and rewarding.

Stick and Rudder: Flying the #4 (Slot Position)

I had the best view in the world as #4. Nobody gets to be as close to as many aircraft as the Slot Pilot. Boss has a great view in front of the formation, but can't see what's happening behind him where the "metal" is very close! The other wingmen are laser-focused on the Boss's jet to maintain position and don't get a great view of anything else. In my position beneath the Boss's tailpipes with #2 and #3 tight on either side, I got to see just how tight the formation was flying and truly got to see the Blue Angels experience up close—VERY close!

Most Difficult Maneuver: Double Farvel

My most challenging maneuver to learn was the Double Farvel, where the 4-plane Diamond flies by the crowd with both #1 and #4 upside down. It would eventually become my favorite maneuver, but only after screwing it up many, many times in training! For some reason, when I rolled the #4 jet upside down, I forgot where the radio switches were and how to make minor corrections while inverted to stay in position. Boss and I were learning it together and solicited help from Doc (#5) who had experience flying inverted the previous year as #6 (Opposing Solo).

Memorable Airshow Story

After finishing our show over San Francisco Bay, we did a surprise flyover of Candlestick Park during an NFL game between the San Francisco 49ers and the St. Louis Rams. The game was televised by Fox Sports and John Madden was so impressed when we came over the stadium lights that he named us MVPs during his annual All-Madden Team television show. If you Google "John Madden and the Blue Angels," you can see the flyover and Madden's excited response for yourself!

My most memorable teamwork story was a bird strike I had that damaged an engine during a Friday practice flight for an airshow in Montreal. The maintenance team and Fat Albert (C-130) pilots sprang into action. They removed the engine, loaded it on Bert, flew to NAS Pensacola to pick up a new engine that our maintenance team back at the hangar had prepared for shipment. Upon arrival, the new engine was loaded, and Bert flew back to Montreal where the mechanics worked through the night and the early morning to install the new engine. V8 (#7) flew a maintenance check flight on the jet that morning and I flew it in the airshow later that day. An incredible example of Blue Angels teamwork, professionalism, and dedication to our mission of flying the best airshow in the world!

FLYING #5 (LEAD SOLO): LCDR RYAN "DOC" SCHOLL, USN

Figure 11 - Solo Pilots performing the Knife-Edge Pass

Description and Responsibilities

My three years with the Blue Angels were hands down the most difficult and the best flying tour of my career! I spent my first year as the #7 (Narrator) and my last two as a solo pilot in the Demo. When Boss Dom arrived, I was the #5 Lead Solo and the Operations Officer managing the Team's long-term plans and the day-to-day activities. In 1997, I was one of the three old salts flying in the demo and my primary duty was ensuring the training and preparation of the #6 Opposing Solo was safe and effective while learning my position as the Lead Solo and flying on the left side of the Delta formation. The six jet demo pilots in 1997 were all very experienced in the F/A-18C, which made for great understanding, patience, and steep learning curves.

The TEAM. "Solo" pilot sounds so individual, but the greatest thing I learned while with the Blue Angels was the value of teamwork. Officially, "the Blues" is organized as a squadron, but they function as a high performing team with the very best enlisted personnel our nation and our Navy and Marine Corps have to offer and 16 of the hardest working officers in the Navy and Marine Corps. As hard as my last year was in time spent working, I treasured every second watching the greatness that is Blue Angel Teamwork on the ground and in the air. It was a thing of beauty. Some use the "duck swimming" analogy, but I will tell you the amount of work to make sure the six demo jets, the 2-seat #7 jet, and the C-130 are fully ready to go and looking pristine is very labor intensive and the result of a whole TEAM effort with everyone giving 100%. It's never all roses and spotless performance, but the deviations were so small that only a trained eye could tell. The constant drive for improvement and for seeking perfection is ingrained in each member of the team, so you know and trust that any mistake will be corrected during the next flight.

Stick and Rudder: Flying the #5 (Lead Solo) Position

Blue Angels Solo pilots spend the first 30 minutes of the demonstration max performing the F/A-18 from -2.5Gs to +7.5Gs (7.5 times the force of gravity), maximum roll rates of the aircraft, and pushing the speed and G-forces to the edges of the allowable maneuvering envelope of the F/A-18. Because we Solos used full stick deflection—full aft, all the way left, all the way right, and full forward, sometimes on the same maneuver—the Diamond pilots affectionately referred to Blue Angels #5 and #6 as "the Piston Brothers."

Most Difficult Maneuver

Being a Piston Brother is NOT helpful once you've joined the 6-plane Delta formation for the final portion of the show. Flying Blue Angel close formation is not easy and there is a transition from dynamic max performance to precise, smooth control that took me a long time to understand. For me, it was a physical and mental transition that had to be accomplished while racing to join Blue Angels #1-#4 in the Diamond formation behind the crowd with no room for delay. Even switching to the left side of the Delta formation from #6 to #5 for my final year in 1997 was hard for me because the turns were now into my position and that required completely different stick and throttle movement, as well as constant smoothness that was only fleeting in the Solos portion of the demo with high speed and high-G maneuvering.

Memorable Airshow Story

Large crowds in big metropolitan areas like Seattle, San Francisco, Chicago and Cleveland made for spectacular shows with fantastic backdrops. I loved 'em. Smaller show sites where it was a little more intimate were personally rewarding for me. The city or town is fully supporting the air show and it takes a lot to make an air show happen. I knew that a great performance was going to touch somebody that may never have seen something like that in their life.

I have to admit, I always wanted my "close to perfect" or best performance to be at the Navy and Marine Master Jet Bases where the Blue Angels recruit seasoned pilots and technicians. It's also where we came from and where we will return. You knew there were discerning eyes watching every maneuver and rendezvous, but our fellow naval aviators also knew the challenges to make a show like that happen. My favorite performance was at Naval Air Station Cecil Field in

Jacksonville, FL. Yogi (#6) and I were on fire, and the Boss was pushing a tight show, so the Delta was brilliant. I think the whole TEAM earned our pay that day.

Another "close to perfect" performance for the Solos was the opening show at Naval Air Facility (NAF) El Centro, CA. While Yogi was nursing a couple cracked ribs from a fall, Utah (#5, Lead Solo the previous year) returned for the opening show and was flying as #6 (Opposing Solo).[13] We were nailing each maneuver, including the very difficult Inverted Tuck Over Roll, a maneuver that challenged Utah and I nearly the whole previous year.

Fat Albert ("Bert"). What a great name for the Blue Angels C-130 that transports the technicians, support officers, parts, and equipment to each show site and puts on a really cool demo that used Jet-Assisted Takeoff (JATO) on the show days. Truly, Bert and her crew were unsung heroes many times at show sites going to get parts or engines, flying through the night, to make sure the demonstration jets were ready to go. The Blue Angels owed a lot to Bert and her Marine Corps crew. They were vital members of "the TEAM."

---

[13] LCDR Mark "Utah" Provo, USN.

FLYING #6 (OPPOSING SOLO): LT SCOTT "YOGI" BEARE, USN

Figure 12 - The Delta formation over USS Constitution

Description and Responsibilities

Each and every day, the Blue Angels represent thousands of aviators, Sailors, and Marines on the front lines of freedom. As ambassadors of naval aviation, all Blue Angels must be responsible for continuing the Team's legacy of excellence. The coveted Blue Angels Crest represents an incredible amount of history and demands excellence from those privileged to wear it and call themselves a Blue Angel.

Along with the Lead Solo (#5), the Opposing Solo (#6) demonstrates the maximum performance characteristics of the F/A-18 Hornet. This includes opposing high-G maneuvers at high speed and very low altitude. In addition, I flew formation aerobatic maneuvers in the 6-plane Delta formation in the right outpost position outboard of Kato (#2).

Stick and Rudder: Flying the #6 (Opposing Solo) Position

Flying as the Opposing Solo required keen stick and rudder skills, attention to detail, and constant situational awareness.

A deep understanding of the aircraft's capabilities and a mastery of advanced flying techniques was necessary to fly the jet safely at low altitude on the edge of the envelope. Understanding the roll divergence of a twin tailed fighter jet during multiple aileron rolls, relying mainly on rudders at near stalling angles of attack to control position, and managing high g-forces without the benefit of a G-suit are just some of the unique skills required of the Opposing Solo. Other skills included discipline in the timing pattern in between maneuvers and aggressive, high speed rendezvouses behind the crowd to set up multi-plane maneuvers.

The timing pattern to set up the opposing maneuvers by #5 and #6 required precise control of airspeed, position over the ground, and timing. Our typical timing pattern was 5,000 feet above the ground, three miles left and right of show center. Referencing stopwatches in our cockpits, we would simultaneously dive our aircraft to an altitude of 200 feet, covering a mile every nine seconds with the goal of meeting exactly over a boat or school bus marking CenterPoint while correcting for the wind and clouds. Stick and rudder skills plus keen mental focus are required to achieve a safe, successful maneuver that thrills the crowd.

Most Difficult Maneuver: Rendezvous for the Delta Roll

By far the most challenging maneuver as #6 was the transition from flying single-plane dynamic solo maneuvers to joining the 6-plane Delta formation. During the show, I spent 30 minutes engaged in violent, high-G, high speed flight; then, I had to join the other jets for the final

15 minutes of the show. This abrupt transition to formation flying was extremely challenging, especially for the first maneuver, the Delta Roll. During Winter Training, the coordination and fine motor skills necessary to execute a very smooth roll while pulling aft stick and trying to stay in position within precise parameters seemed to elude me. Numerous flights in training and throughout the airshow season allowed me to develop muscle memory, confidence, and success, but this maneuver always demanded extra effort.

Completing the first portion of the show, Doc (#5) and I would clear the flight line after our last solo maneuver. I would visually acquire the Diamond formation behind the crowd, select afterburner, accelerate to 500 knots, and set up my rendezvous. There is very little time to execute the rendezvous that required high closure speeds of 200 mph at low altitude, then rapid deceleration with high-Gs for a controlled cross under to the right side of the formation. Completing the rendezvous just as the Boss was ready to begin the Delta Roll, I often struggled to get blood back in my head from the high-G deceleration using opposite rudder and aileron. I'd take a breath to force myself to settle down and focus on flying my "paint" on Kato's (#2) jet as we started to climb and roll. Flying the rendezvous successfully and safely was as challenging as flying the maneuver.

Memorable Airshow Story

My most memorable memory (of many) of the 1997 season was our flyover of "Old Ironsides," the USS Constitution on her 200th anniversary. Completing a 3.5 year, $12 million restoration, the USS Constitution unfurled her sails off the coast of Massachusetts on July 21, 1997. She set sail that day for the first time in 116 years. With a 20th century escort of Navy ships and bagpipes playing on deck, we flew overhead to salute a ship that never lost a battle in 84 years of active duty. A fitting tribute for an old warrior. I was honored to have been part of the Blue Angels tasked that day with rendering honors. I remember fighting the urge to sightsee as it seemed we barely cleared her mast as the cannons fired a broadside beneath us.

In second place is my memorable guest appearance with Sesame Street's Elmo in Grand Junction, CO. On that day in September 1997, I found myself at the end of the runway in deep thought and conversation with a furry red Muppet. In the words of Dave "Griff" Griffith, our honorary Blue Angel friend: "Priceless!"

FLYING FAT ALBERT: MAJ STU "BEEF" SMITH, USMC

Figure 13 - The Blue Angels C-130 Hercules, "Fat Albert"

Description and Responsibilities

Our primary mission was to safely transport the support personnel—highly trained Sailors and Marines— and their equipment to Winter Training and the show sites throughout the airshow season. Our secondary mission was to demonstrate the maneuverability and unique capabilities of the C-130 Hercules. Affectionately named "Fat Albert," the demonstration included a dynamic, fiery takeoff maneuver using Jet-Assisted Takeoff bottles (JATO)!

Being Marine-1 (M1) on the Blue Angels was amazing. I felt I was the CO of the Bert Office, an all-Marine Team consisting of three pilots, a navigator, loadmaster, two flight engineers, and a maintenance technician. Our camaraderie and trust were inspiring. I was responsible for the C-130's maintenance, winter visits, pre-season simulator training, training flights, and flight planning to each show site during the season. The year prior, I coordinated a loaner C-130 from a USMC squadron while "Bert" was out of service completing a scheduled heavy maintenance inspection and repair. We didn't miss a single airshow or logistics mission with the loaner aircraft. As we were getting short on JATO bottles, and new ones cost $2000 each. I found 5,000 bottles stored in a depot that we could recertify for $250 a bottle, saving the Navy over four million dollars.

Flying the Fat Albert C-130 Flight Demonstration

The Bert Demo is designed to show the crowd how USMC C-130s can operate from short expeditionary runways while avoiding enemy small arms fire. It consists of a max performance JATO climbing at a 45-degree angle to several thousand feet and a high-speed pass at 100 feet before climbing to end the show with a simulated Tactical Landing Zone (TLZ) landing—a steep approach designed to avoid enemy fire and a short field landing to stop precisely in front of the crowd.

The crew coordination during the entire demo, especially the JATO, is amazing— it's a textbook example of a flight crew working in close coordination. While the Pilot is busy flying the plane, the Co-Pilot calls out the aircraft's airspeed, altitude, and attitude; the Flight Engineer monitors engine performance and adjusting power, and takes over the

Co-Pilot's calls when the two pilots transition to visually scanning outside the aircraft. The Navigator times the firing of the JATO bottles and calls for the Pilot to pushover to level flight at exactly 11 seconds. The First Mech and Load Master monitor the JATO bottles.

These calls and procedures are practiced during simulator training and numerous practice profiles. The sim training is critical to refining the normal procedures and practicing emergencies. For example, we simulated a JATO bottle coming off the aircraft during the pushover maneuver and damaging two engines on one side. Because of the low airspeed at pushover (97 knots), it is critical to respond quickly and correctly to maintain control of the aircraft. By the time we completed simulator training, the pilots had mastered these techniques. The High-Speed Pass and TLZ landing are more of the same, with great crew coordination.

Memorable Airshow Story

Every airshow was amazing, and seeing America from state to state was spectacular. Meeting the public at these show sites was the best part. Having a home show in front of family and friends was exciting and very busy. Going to speak at my high school and seeing my former teachers was inspiring and humbling at the same time. The sense of pride in being on the team. This is such a unique environment. You go from a regular civilian to a rockstar with the zip of a flight suit. The sense of pride, teamwork, and professionalism that the Blue Angels represent is AMAZING. We are just lucky enough to wear the Blue Angels flight suit for our tour and try to uphold those standards. Another unique opportunity is how we are able to affect and inspire others with the platform we have during our time.

One of the most amazing things I witnessed while on the team was when Dingo (Capt. Darren "Dingo" Martin, USMC, M2) and I visited a half-way house for homeless teens in San Diego. I introduced myself and said, "The next guy to talk to you lived in a half-way house not long ago." Dingo told his story of how difficult it was and described some of the decisions he was faced with. One time, a bunch of his buddies were planning to steal the local van and he chose not to go. Ultimately, his buddies all got kicked out of the house. He also talked about one of his best days as a teen, when he found a pair of shoes in a dumpster—and they actually fit. The 17 kids swarmed him after his testimonial. He stayed in contact with many of them and some pulled themselves out of their situation. It still gives me shivers thinking about what I witnessed!

APPENDIX III
1997–1998 BLUE ANGELS

F/A-18 DEMONSTRATION PILOTS

#1 Capt George Dom, USN (1997-98)

#2 Maj Pat Cooke, USMC (1997)

#2 Maj Scott Wedemeyer, USMC (1998)

#3/#4 LtCdr Mark Dunleavy, USN (1997-98)

#3 LtCdr Dave Silkey, USN (1998)

#4 LtCdr Scott Moyer, USN (1997)

#5 LtCdr Ryan Scholl, USN (1997)

#6/#5 LtCdr Scott Beare, USN (1997-98)

#7/#6 Lt. Doug Verissimo, USN (1997-98)

NARRATOR/MEDIA FLIGHTS

#7 Lt. Scott Ind, USN (1998)

FAT ALBERT AIRLINES / FLIGHT DEMONSTRATION

Maj. Stuart Smith, USMC (1997)

Capt. Darren Martin, USMC (1997-98)

Capt. Robert Wunderlich, USMC (1997)

Capt. Dwight Neeley, USMC (1998)

MSgt Steve Ward, USMC

MSgt Theodore Veit, USMC

Gsgt David Files, USMC

SSgt Darrell Carter, USMC

SSgt Scott Esche, USMC

SSgt Randy Richter, USMC

SSgt Scott Tucker, USMC

SUPPORT OFFICERS

#8 Lt Kevin Lacasse, USN - Events Coordinator (1997-98)

Lt Clark Merritt, USN - Maintenance Officer (1997)

Lt Neal Austin, USN - Maintenance Officer (1998)

Lt Bryan Buchanan, USN - Flight Surgeon (1997-98)

LtCdr Patricia Tezak, USN - Admin Officer (1997)

LtCdr Nancy Lake, USN - Admin Officer (1998)

LtCdr John Kirby, USN - Public Affairs Officer (1997)

Lt Tanya Wallace, USN - Public Affairs Officer (1998)

Lt Duke Heinz, USN - Supply Officer (1997)

Lt Michelle Saari, USN - Supply Officer (1998)

SENIOR ENLISTED LEADERS

MMC: AVCM(AW) Dennis Therkildsen, USN

CMC: AVCM(AW/NAC) Joseph Colbert, USN

CMC: AWCM(AW/SW/NAC) Scott Carmean, USN

CREW COORDINATORS ("FRONTMEN")

AD1(AW) Foster Stringer, USN

AS1(AW) R.C. Hirn, USN

AD1(AW) Steve Hudson, USN

ADMINISTRATION

YN1(AW) Chris Adams, USN

AD1(AW) Chuck Ignarski, USN

AT1(AW) Ed Engel, USN

YN2 Joe Marshall, USN

YN3 Geof Allen, USN

AT1(AW) Ed Engel, USN

PR1(AW) Demetrius Seowtewa, USN

AOAN William Palmer, USN

AEAN Jason Stokes, USN

AKAN Jonathan Munger, USN

AN William McGhee, USN

AN Andrew Basha, USN

AN Roland Foskey, USN

AN Jennifer Brown, USN

AN Julie Kozub, USN

AA Guadalupe Villalobos, USN

AIRFRAMES

AMS1 Michael Clouse, USN

SSgt Jeff Stafford, USMC

AMH1(AW) David Shaw, USN

SSgt Doug Maile, USMC

AMS1(AW) Kinscem Danzie, USN

AMS2 Todd Campbell, USN

AMS2(AW) Mike Schurb, USN

AMH2 Tony Scott, USN

AMH2(AW) Scott Whitworth, USN

AMH2 John Squires, USN

AMS2 Todd Czubinski, USN

AMS2(AW) Greg Semo, USN

AMS2 Jeff Lange, USN

AMH2(AW) Gary Supeck, Jr., USN

AMH2(AW) Keith Carter, USN

AVIONICS

AT1(AW) Todd Buczek, USN

SSgt Jeffrey Barber, USMC

AE1(AW) Tim Rice, USN

AT1(AW/SW) Joseph Hurley, USN

AE1(AW) Brian DuFour, USN

AE1(AW) Thomas Vittitow, USN

SSgt Jessie Chacon, USMC

AT2(AW/NAC) John Scheck, USN

AT2 Steve Pinette, USN

AE2 Gus Pacheco, USN

AT2 Rodney Rose, USN

AT2(AW) Marc Scott, USN

Sgt Christopher Calhoun, USMC

AE2 Brian Koendarfer, USN

AE3(AW) Chris Smith, USN

CREW CHIEFS

AMH1(AW) George Hadley, USN

AO1(AW) Derrick Robinson, USN

AS1(AW) Kirk Klawitter, USN

AE1(AW) James Thompson, USN

AS1 Peter Ford, USN

AMH1(AW) Kenneth Thomas, USN

AE1 Karen Marini, USN

AMH2(AW) Rick Boswell, USN

AMS2(AW) David Gonsalves, USN

AO2 Terrance Williams, USN

Sgt Charlie Clark, USMC

AMH2 Lewis Freeman, USN

AO2(AW) Chris Simmons, USN

AMS2 Shane Owens, USN

AT2 Edward Primeau, USN

PR2(AW) Mark Vecchioni, USN

AD2 Alfredo Acevedo, USN

AE2(AW) Jay Hersh, USN

AS2 LeJuan Clay, USN

COMMAND CAREER COUNSELOR

AE1(AW) Frank Maciag, USN

EVENTS COORDINATION

YN2 Frank Campbell, USN

YN2 Erick Winford, USN

YN2 Jason Durnell, USN

LIFE SUPPORT

AME1(AW) Ed Pennycook, USN

AME2 Jeffrey Ferraer, USN

PR2(AW) Brian Hawkins, USN

AME2(AW) Jacqueline Fauria, USN

PR2 Steve Christie, USN

AME2 Brian Tennyson, USN

AME2 Mike Steele, USN

PR2(AW) John Beach, USN

MAINTENANCE CONTROL

ADCS(AW) Craig Narramore, USN

ATC(AW) Bill Daniels, USN

AZC(AW) Scott Johnson, USN

AZC(AW) Mike Odom, USN

AEC(AW) Robert Wilson, USN

GySgt Kyle Ziegler, USMC

AZ1(AW) David Bontrager, USN

AZ2(AW) Bill Whittington, Jr., USN

AZ2(AW) Ronald Bourne, USN

AZ2(AW) Dana Moser, USN

MEDICAL

HM2(CAC) Brian Hashey, USN

HM2(AW) David Greenier, USN

HM2 Corey Coldiron, USN

PAINT SHOP

AMS2(AW) Paul Beaumont, USN

AMH1 Everett McGinnis, USN

AMH2 Stephen Miller, USN

AMS2(NAC) Ronald Maggi, USN

AT2 Steve Pinette, USN

AMH2(AW) William Schomer, USN

AE2 Victor Melendez, USN

AD2 Michael Gause, USN

YNSA Samson Liburd, USN

POWER PLANTS

AD1(AW) Daniel Robinson, USN

SSgt Vic Schroeder, USMC

AD1(AW) Dominic Colao, USN

AD1 Kevin Schmid, USN

AD1(AW) Raymond LaVigne, USN

AD2 Thomas Hunter, USN

Sgt Leon Keys, USMC

AD2 Paul Burris, USN

Sgt John Carr, USMC

AD3 Casey Jones, USN

PUBLIC AFFAIRS

PH1(NAC) Casey Akins, USN

PH1(SW) Ronnie Newsome, USN

DM1(AW) Eulogio Devera, USN

DM2 Keith Wilson, USN

PH2 Glenn Sircy, USN

DM2 Mario Hair, USN

JO2(SW) Dave Fitz, USN

QUALITY ASSURANCE

AMS1(AW) Jerry Czubinski, USN

AME1(AW) Brian DeRitter, USN

AD1 Earl Purifoy, USN

AT1(AW) Jose Acevedo, USN

AME1(AW) Michael Graham, USN

AZ2(AW) Ronald Bourne, USN

AD2(AW) Michael Gonzales, USN

AZ2 Kevin Muegerl, USN

SUPPLY

AK1(AW) Edward Rhodes, USN

AK1(AW) Renee Kaufman, USN

AK1(AW) David Lee, USN

AK1 Gary Walker, USN

AK2 Brad Dark, USN

AK2(AW) Robert Muretta, USN

AK2 Jeff Wells, USN

AK2(AW) Scott Leaver, USN

AK2(AW) Jonathan Williams, USN

AK2(AW) Tim King, USN

AK2(AW) Jack Bailey, USN

AK3 Cher Olson, USN

VIDEO

AE2 Joey Thomas, USN

AT2 Anthony Smith, USN

AE2 Fanandus Ballard, USN

AMH2 John Squires, USN

AT2(AW/SW) Jonathan Greer, USN

OMBUDSMEN

Ms. Sherri Hirn

Ms. Kathy Wunderlich

MCDONNELL DOUGLAS/BOEING TECH REPS

Mr. Bill Ahlstrom

Mr. Jerry Lienhop

Mr. Don Rodgers

Mr. Dick Tuschinski

DEPARTMENT OF THE NAVY

Ms. Alicia Petruska

Acknowledgements

Brian Schwartz for shepherding me through the book publishing process.

Daniel Siuba for his detailed editorial comments.

Jim Loehr for his friendship and enthusiastic encouragement.

Russ Bartlett, Scott Beare, Pat Cooke, Jenny Evans, Nancy Lotinsky, Scott Moyer, and Stu Smith for helpful comments on the manuscript.

My 1997 wingmen for sharing their thoughts in Appendix II: Pat "Kato" Cooke, Mark "Gucci" Dunleavy, Scott "Scooter" Moyer, Ryan "Doc" Scholl, Scott "Yogi" Beare, and Stu "Beef" Smith.

Krystyn Hartman for our early collaboration and her belief in the power of high-trust relationships.

Tom Davin, Parker Kuldau, Ryan Nothhaft, and Michelle Saari for detailed comments on the cover design.

My wife, Rian, for her love and support as my steadfast truth-teller.

Our daughters, Livi and Denna, each blazing their own paths. I can't wait to see what's next.

To the amazing naval aviators, naval flight officers, chief petty officers, maintenance techs, and shipmates I had the unbelievably good fortune to serve and sacrifice with at sea and ashore in defense of America and our allies. I learned from each of you.

The Chiefs of Naval Aviation Training during my tour with the Blue Angels: RDML William "Tball" Hayden, RADM Michael "Shooter" Bowman, and RADM Michael "Smiles" Bucchi. All three were HIGH-TRUST Leaders who supported us 100% and trusted us to carry out our mission as we saw fit.

To my friends and colleagues at ACI Jet, a special place to work in a special place to live.

www.ingramcontent.com/pod-product-compliance
Lightning Source LLC
Chambersburg PA
CBHW071606210326
41597CB00019B/3427